DOING PHENOMENOGRAPHY

Creative Research Methods in Practice

Series Editor: **Helen Kara**, We Research It Ltd.

This dynamic series presents short practical books by and for researchers around the world on how to use creative and innovative research methods from apps to zines. Edited by the leading independent researcher Helen Kara, it is the first series to provide guidance on using creative research methods across all disciplines.

Find out more at
bristoluniversitypress.co.uk/
creative-research-methods-in-practice

DOING PHENOMENOGRAPHY

A Practical Guide

Amanda M.L. Taylor-Beswick and Eva Hornung

With a Foreword by
Sheila Webber

First published in Great Britain in 2024 by

Policy Press, an imprint of
Bristol University Press
University of Bristol
1–9 Old Park Hill
Bristol
BS2 8BB
UK
t: +44 (0)117 374 6645
e: bup-info@bristol.ac.uk

Details of international sales and distribution partners are available at
policy.bristoluniversitypress.co.uk

© Bristol University Press 2024

British Library Cataloguing in Publication Data
A catalogue record for this book is available from the British Library

ISBN 978-1-4473-6989-9 hardcover
ISBN 978-1-4473-6990-5 paperback
ISBN 978-1-4473-6991-2 ePub
ISBN 978-1-4473-6992-9 ePdf

The right of Amanda M.L. Taylor-Beswick and Eva Hornung to be identified as authors of this work has been asserted by them in accordance with the Copyright, Designs and Patents Act 1988.

All rights reserved: no part of this publication may be reproduced, stored in a retrieval system, or transmitted in any form or by any means, electronic, mechanical, photocopying, recording, or otherwise without the prior permission of Bristol University Press.

Every reasonable effort has been made to obtain permission to reproduce copyrighted material. If, however, anyone knows of an oversight, please contact the publisher.

The statements and opinions contained within this publication are solely those of the authors and not of the University of Bristol or Bristol University Press. The University of Bristol and Bristol University Press disclaim responsibility for any injury to persons or property resulting from any material published in this publication.

Bristol University Press and Policy Press work to counter discrimination on grounds of gender, race, disability, age and sexuality.

Cover design: Qube Design
Front cover image: iStock/Veronika Oliinyk

Contents

List of figures, tables and boxes	vi
About the authors	viii
Acknowledgements	x
Foreword by Sheila Webber	xii

1	Why phenomenography and why now	1
2	Introducing phenomenography	11
3	Research design and ethics in phenomenographic work	31
4	Data generation in phenomenographic work	51
5	Phenomenographic transcription and data analysis	69
6	Presenting the findings of phenomenographic work	91
7	Conclusion	109

Additional resources	115
References	117
Index	141

List of figures, tables and boxes

Figures

2.1	The experience of learning	27
3.1	Phenomenography methodology	33
4.1	Focusing activity	55
4.2	Completed focusing activity	56
5.1	Phenomenographic relationality	73
5.2	Log book page	80
5.3	Index of colour code	82
5.4	Colour coding statements	83
5.5	Interview number at each statement	84
5.6	Cutting the interviews along statements	85
6.1	Outcome space	92
6.2	Hierarchy of categories	100
6.3	Outcome space	103
6.4	'How' and 'what' outcome space	104
6.5	Outcome space: conceptions of professional skills in pictorial form	107

Tables

5.1	Emerging categories of description: early stage formulation of category 1	86
6.1	Outcome space 1	99
6.2	Outcome space 2	100
6.3	Outcome space: conceptions of professional skills	106

Boxes

3.1	Practical guidelines for the conduct of phenomenographic research	34

3.2	Phenomenographic study design in a doctoral thesis	35
3.3	Phenomenographic study rationale in a doctoral thesis	36
3.4	Ethical issues at seven research stages	41
4.1	Developing research and interview questions	59
4.2	Interview schedule	62
5.1	Transcription and analysis rationale	71
6.1	Categories of description	93
6.2	Categories of description	96
6.3	Example overview of dimensions of variation	96
6.4	Use of vignettes	101

About the authors

Amanda M.L. Taylor-Beswick is the founding director of the Centre for Digital Transformation at the University of Cumbria, where during the writing of this book she was successful in her claim to conferment to the title of professor. Amanda's background is as a social worker and social scientist, practising in Northern Ireland's integrated Health and Social Care environment. Amanda moved to England in 2007 to pursue a career in social work academia, returning to Ireland in the months preceding the 2020 global health crisis, to take up an academic position in the School of Social Science, Education and Social Work, at Queen's University Belfast, with a teaching and research focus on digital and sociotechnical intersections. Amanda is well-known for her work on the digital as associated with the social and has many awards for her innovative approaches to teaching, learning and research. Including her 'glocal' (local and global) social work book group, that continues to provide a connecting space for learning, for social scientists, from across many disciplines and in multiple jurisdictions. Amongst the various roles Amanda holds, she is extremely proud to be part of the phenomenography research community and to be a volunteer at Carlisle Youth Zone, where she works closely with the Youth Voice group to ensure that the experiences of young people are front and centre in shaping youth work and other services and approaches in Cumbria.

Eva Hornung manages a one-person research library in the adult and further education sector in Dublin. After qualifying as a librarian in 1995 she worked in a public library in Germany. In 2001 she moved to Ireland to pursue a Master's in Library and Information Studies. She has used phenomenography both for her doctorate in Information Studies, which won a highly commended award at the Emerald/EFMD Outstanding Doctoral

Research Awards in 2011, and for her Master's in Education. Eva is an active member of the Library Association of Ireland (currently chairing the continuing professional development committee) and of the Chartered Institute of Library and Information Professionals, where she acts as mentor for professional awards. She has delivered guest lectures in Ireland and the United Kingdom and presented extensively, including at European Association for Research on Learning and Instruction (EARLI) and European Association for Practitioner Research on Improving Learning (EAPRIL) conferences. She wrote this book in a personal capacity.

Acknowledgements

Amanda M.L. Taylor-Beswick: No piece of academic work truly happens in isolation of others. Others in this instance, for me and this work, are wide and varied, and include Helen Kara, the series editor, a long-standing and wholesome academic friend. Candice Satchwell, my doctoral supervisor, who introduced me to and guided me through my early years as a phenomenographic researcher, and the students who came forward to make my doctoral work possible. Julie Mennell, Vice Chancellor of the University of Cumbria, who provides the context in which academic work such as this can be realised. My wife, Caroline Taylor-Beswick, who is relentless in her support of me, my life choices and my work. Including my more recent rescue of a wonderful greyhound, Luca, through the lovely Joanna Link and with much encouragement from my dear friend Fiona McClenaghan. There are many many others I could mention, in particular my son Ben, those that have set their stake with my stake throughout my field practice, research and academic years. To each of you, and you will know who you are, I am and will be forever profoundly grateful. And of course, my wonderfully generous, kind and humorous coauthor, Eva Hornung, who, since way back when, has been a rich and consistent source of academic rigour and academic soul food. During the writing of this book I lost my sister Ann, and so I conclude my dedication with a deep value for all that she was, to me, and to the world.

Eva Hornung: The best thing about co-authoring this book was that I could collaborate with my friend, Amanda Taylor-Beswick. She had the idea and invited me along. Amanda is not only an inspiring scholar, but, more importantly, a fabulous human being with a big heart. Early morning (yawn!) Teams meetings could only be endured because I knew she would pop up on the screen with a big smile. Big thanks go to my ever-supporting family and friends, who had to listen to another of my mad ideas – yet again! Sheila Webber, my doctoral supervisor, provided the spark that lit the candle. Her own academic work encouraged me to join the wonderful phenomenographic community and I found my research tribe when I attended my first EARLI SIG 9 conference in Kristianstad in 2008.

We would like to collectively express our gratitude to the individuals who contributed significantly to our project. First, heartfelt thanks to the proposal reviewers for dedicating their time and offering valuable guidance. A special acknowledgment is reserved for the manuscript reviewer, whose meticulous feedback played a crucial role in enhancing the quality of our book. Helen Kara deserves special recognition for her pivotal role as a guide and mentor throughout the publishing process. Her consistent encouragement and guidance have been invaluable, and we are sincerely thankful for her unwavering support. Our appreciation also extends to everyone at Policy Press, and to the PhD students and phenomenographers who generously granted permission to reference their work and models. We genuinely hope that our representation accurately reflects the essence of their contributions. Lastly, a special mention goes to Sheila, who wrote the Foreword; your kindness and significant contribution are greatly appreciated by both of us.

Foreword

Sheila Webber, Senior Lecturer & Head of Libraries, Information & Society Research Group, Information School, The University of Sheffield

Welcome to this valuable addition to the qualitative research methods literature. Whether you are exploring phenomenography for the first time, or already identify yourself as a phenomenographer, you will enjoy the pages that lie in front of you. I hold phenomenography close to my heart. I can still remember the moment when I first truly felt I could call myself *a researcher*, and that was standing in front of a much-scrawled flipchart as data, meanings and relationships crystallised and I felt that phenomenographic 'aha' moment. It came after much immersion, reflection, organisation, argument, mapping, revision … and the journey certainly didn't end with 'aha'! However, it was an enriching journey in which I learnt about myself and my fellow researchers, as well as about the participants who shared their stories.

What I lacked, though, was a concise, practical guide to phenomenography. As the authors explain in Chapter 2, there is a rich body of literature giving accounts of phenomenography and various aspects of the approach. This includes essential readings from phenomenography's founders. Nevertheless, this literature has not included an introductory textbook. The nearest has been Bowden and Green (2005) which is not easy to get hold of, and which also provides shafts of light on the research process, rather than a systematic guide. Therefore, this volume is very welcome.

Phenomenography is in some ways an easy research approach to define: it has to start with a question about variation, you have to capture your chosen sample's experience or conception of a phenomenon, and you have to end up with categories of description and an outcome space. However, there is a huge leap from staring at a pile or folder of interview transcripts and presenting your findings in the required format. As is illustrated in Chapters 5 and 6, there are many ways of getting from this A to B, and you have to find the one that works for you and your data, but still, this has to be a rigorous process of analysis. From that perspective I found Chapters 5 and 6 (on analysis and presentation) particularly useful.

It is also very helpful to remind oneself where phenomenography originated (see Chapter 2). Marton (1992) recalls his own 'aha' moment, when his PhD viva examiner on the one hand said Marton's PhD was flawless, and on the other questioned whether it really had 'increased our understanding of what it takes to learn in our everyday reality'. This set Marton directly onto the path of co-developing phenomenography. Whilst phenomenography has been adopted into a huge range of disciplinary contexts beyond education, it is still a channel for learning about ourselves and others, and (as the authors of this book say) helping 'develop the world in ways that we all can individually and collaboratively better exist'.

1

Why phenomenography and why now

Phenomenography is a multimodal research approach that increasingly makes use of creative, arts-based, digital and embodied methods. It has participatory and ethical elements and is potentially transformative. This book will provide a step-by-step guide through this complex and rewarding approach to research. Although phenomenography is still developing, we have reached the exciting point of being able to provide an overview of the method in practice, through this long-awaited guide to its use. We will set out the key principles and practices established to date and show you how to use this method in your own research.

Whilst throughout this book we refer to and make comment on the relevance of phenomenographic research work to a range of fields and disciplinary areas, it is important to note phenomenography origins in higher education (Marton and Säljö 1976a). A method designed to help educators and educational designers to understand and progress pedagogy, learning processes, and practices. Given its origins, it feels pertinent to comment on the troublesome state of higher education, in the context of what we believe phenomenography has to offer. Issues for the sector have been accelerated by the COVID-19 pandemic, involving technological innovation and developments, which continue to raise challenging questions about the currency and effectiveness of the traditional model of higher education, higher education pedagogies, and research practices. Issues that had been brought into focus pre-COVID-19 pandemic by authors such as Susskind and Susskind (2015: 1), who at that time were stressing how humanity was on 'the brink of a period of fundamental and irreversible change in the way that the expertise of specialists is made available to society [and that] technology will be the main driver of this change.'. They make the point that 'professions are not immutable' and that 'the professions in their current form will no longer be the best answer' to all the needs of a society that has become even more technology saturated. They appropriately challenge professions and professionals to take a more strategic and open approach 'to the possibility of change in their own disciplines.'. Stressing how the unprecedented abundance of knowledge, made possible through the Internet, challenges the whole idea of and need for 'expertise' (Taylor-Beswick 2019: 135).

Long gone are the days of the 'Sage on the Stage' (King 1993: 30) or the educator/professor/researcher as sole custodian of learning, knowledge and knowledge creation. There now exists a much more acute need to listen in the world more broadly, and to lean into the many and current unknowns and uncertainties. The looking and working into the future of higher education and research practices being just some of them. Phenomenography offers a method of listening, making sense of, and developing responses and possible solutions to what people tell us they experience based on how people tell us they are experiencing various, and often vital, phenomena.

Furthermore, while there are a 'huge range of creative research methods available to researchers' (Kara 2020: 1), a review of research methods literature (for example, Cohen et al 2017; Patten 2017; Cresswell 2022) illuminates a notable absence or dearth of reference to phenomenography or inclusion of the rich tapestry of phenomenographic literature. This is an issue we each experienced as early career researchers and just one of the reasons underpinning our individual and collective reasons to write this book. These motivations are overwhelmingly grounded in our experiences of learning how to *do* phenomenography, our experiences of *becoming* phenomenographers, and our experiences of becoming part of the vastly expert phenomenographic research community.

Linked to this is how we connected and our early interactions as new, curious and slightly naïve phenomenographic researchers, mediated through our attendance at the annual European Association for Research on Learning and Instruction's

Phenomenography Special Interest Group (SIG) event, held at the University of Birmingham, UK (Davis et al 2019). The concentrated nature of this event meant that we had the luxury of immersing ourselves in phenomenographic research with a variety of other new and well established phenomenographers. We spent a significant amount of time at this event deliberating and debating 'how to do phenomenography' and sharing the tensions and tribulations we were all experiencing about 'how to do it right'. Our shared and collective angst worsened when bearing witness to the rigour of academic questioning and debate throughout this conference event, which involved many and robust challenges on the design, application and development of this research approach. On reflection, we now recognise that it was this experience that formed part of our urgency to understand more about phenomenography, to get a better grasp of it, and to learn more about how to 'do it right'.

Sin (2010: 306), an established phenomenographer, captured the significance of being involved with and engaging in critique and debate of this nature, explaining how 'readers within an academic community have to be convinced of the quality in a piece of research when they evaluate it against criteria for quality that have been developed through contributions and agreements within that community over time'. This is particularly relevant given that Tight's evaluation of phenomenographic work highlighted how 'it has become more and more obvious that there are considerable variations in practice amongst Phenomenographers' (2016: 325). However, and as noted by Cope (2004: 9), 'if individuals experience phenomena in the world in different ways, why shouldn't different researchers investigating the phenomena of variations in a group of individuals experience the variation in different ways'. Experiences of the phenomenographic SIG community are therefore to be embraced, even though they can at first seem – and be experienced as – quite daunting. In a way *becoming* in and through the research community embodies a significant feature of phenomenographic work, 'communicative validity', a process that involves 'the persuasiveness of researchers regarding the appropriateness of their research methods and final interpretations as judged by the relevant research community' (Van Rossum and Hamer 2010: 47).

Since that time, and through the writing of this book, the authors have only ever connected when either of them has had a question, dilemma or tension relating to the phenomenographic research approach. This also signals the 'why phenomenography and why now' in this work, and our collective belief in the usefulness of a more practical guide or practice handbook. This issue is acknowledged more widely by PhD students and phenomenographic researchers alike. For example, Åkerlind (2005a), a prolific and renowned phenomenographer, when reflecting on her journey into phenomenography as a doctoral student, lamented the lack of literature describing methodological requirements for conducting such research, pointing out that the theoretical basis for phenomenographic research had only been tackled in any depth by Marton and Booth (1997) in their seminal work. Ten years later, Smith (2015: 88) commented in her PhD thesis how 'a further disadvantage of the phenomenographic approach is that there is no manual of phenomenographic method. The absence of a comprehensive guide makes engaging in this research approach a challenging undertaking'. An issue echoed in the even more recent doctoral work of Denholm (2023: 66) who, when trying to learn how to do phenomenography, found that the 'authoritative sources are limited in number'. All of this illustrates how acquiring the skills and abilities to do phenomenographic research comes primarily through significant and independent combing of journal articles that refer to the approach. This book therefore aims to condense the main tenets of the phenomenographic approach in a single comprehensive resource.

Phenomenography as a journey

When setting out on our doctoral journeys we were each keenly aware of the need to broaden and deepen our knowledge of research approaches, including of those less familiar or less well-known methods and methodologies. Fortuitously, we were supervised by directors of studies who actively encouraged and supported our inquisitiveness and curiosities, and who – after listening to our research project aspirations – brought phenomenography to our respective attentions. We have since reflected on how our earliest conversations included reference to how the approach coalesced robustly with the ideas we each had about creating spaces in which research participants could describe an aspect of, or describe an experience in, higher education and workplace learning. Our focus was to gain insights that would support a more refined and authentic understanding linked to professional development as well as pedagogic practice improvement. This is a framing that our supervisors supported us to recognise, which was reflective of the origins and purpose of phenomenographic research. Accordingly, our individual phenomenographic doctoral studies (which we will refer to throughout this book) were designed to first identify and then articulate described experiences of phenomena in social work education and library studies, respectively, fields that form part of the social sciences.

Through our academic work, which includes curriculum design, teaching and supervising research students, we are reminded of the persistent lack of understanding about the place and value of the phenomenographic approach. This is another reason underpinning the 'why phenomenography and why now', and for a practical guide or handbook to support learning about how to *do* phenomenography, that one could reach for, like we do with each other, when questions about doing phenomenography arise. We do not claim that a book of this nature will fully resolve this issue nor settle what Tight (2016) pointed out about increasing variation in the approach taken, referred to earlier. We do, however, believe that learning from how others engage in phenomenographic work can provide a rich resource for new and early stage career researchers. Additionally, due to the number of phenomenographic studies that now exist and the variation in practice as described by Tight and others (for example, Entwistle 1997; Bowden and Walsh 2000; Åkerlind 2005d; Denholm 2023), a practical guide that will reference many of the core and other published works provides a useful starting point for reviewing the appropriateness and relevance of the approach for researchers.

We write this book as post-doctoral phenomenographic researchers, and this book reflects what we have learnt and continue to learn through our research, our involvement, and interactions with other phenomenographic researchers. It is witness to the need for and benefits of a connection with your research community of practice, as noted by others, including Sin (2010). We hope to inspire other researchers to explore and engage with the approach and aim to provide support to overcome some of the obstacles and or challenges we encountered, through the sharing of our journey, our learning, phenomenographic literatures, explanations of phenomenography, and examples drawn from ours and others' phenomenographic work. As already noted, we do not claim or seek to overclaim to have written the ultimate book on doing phenomenographic research, this book is simply a reflection on how we, and others, are using this research approach, including the issues we came upon. There are many other ways of conducting a phenomenographic project and we appreciate that some researchers may disagree or differentiate from the steps and guidance we found helpful or took. Our overriding desire is that, by providing examples of and excerpts of our own work and the work of others, we can encourage current students and academics to consider the range of phenomenography applications when progressing their own studies.

For us, phenomenography is also a philosophy, one that centres on developing our understanding of how things are connected and how we experience the world. We invite readers to invest time immersed in the thinking that developed the approach and that is still informing the approach now; how it was envisaged by the early pioneers and the scholars who have since developed it further. We include a substantial bibliography and many significant and recent studies, in an attempt to highlight how students, academics and practitioners have interpreted phenomenographic principles and applied them in their research work. We each have found examining the multiple ways in which phenomenographic research work has been done to be both encouraging and fascinating, and indeed a phenomenon in and of itself worth phenomenographic analysis! As acknowledged and taken forward by Tight (nd), in his work, *A Phenomenography of Phenomenography*, that ends with the provocation, 'so why, then, persist with phenomenography?' To which we, and many others might reply, because of how well it unpacks experience, so to understand experience much more closely from another's point of view. Notwithstanding different data collection methods and displaying of outcomes, at the core of all this scholarly output is clearly a desire to embed phenomenography firmly in the canon of research methods and approaches. The fact that hundreds of researchers around the world have used it over the past 50 years shows how phenomenography has made a valid contribution to helping answer the many questions humans have about themselves and the world in which they live.

Phenomenography was developed to investigate how learners learn or experience their learning, and it has been used in hundreds of educational studies and other fields since. A renewed focus on the needs of our students, such as creating space for the learner voice, recognising the need for universal design for learning, and finding ways to tackle the climate crisis, to name but a few, leads us to promote this approach to a wider audience. Furthermore, phenomenography has been used in a wide range of academic subject areas, such as social work, library and information studies, management studies, nursing, physics, finance, business, engineering, and medicine.

Overview of contents

As previously noted, the emphasis of this publication is on the practical steps involved, those that we and many others have deployed, when engaged in designing and doing phenomenographic research work. In many respects it is the book we wish we'd had when first encountering phenomenography.

Chapter 2 acknowledges the people who first posed the questions which led them to craft, test and articulate what was, at that time, a novel approach, and brings to attention a selection of the phenomenographers and phenomenographic work that have subsequently shaped and progressed it. The terminology associated with phenomenography is often found to be confused and confusing, with different researchers using terms in a variety of ways, some of which are – or can seem to be – contradictory. We have chosen to go back to the founders, the original sources, to disentangle some of this confusion. But as you will see, a certain flexibility is permitted, and it might be that you too will bring your own angle to the approach in your application and future articulations.

We then move, in Chapter 3, to the design and designing of phenomenographic studies and, linked to this, some tangible and possible ethical questions and tensions. Qualitative research calls for close relationships between researchers, the participants and the data created. If you, the reader, have experience of qualitative research, you will be quite familiar with many of these steps, yet much of what we outline is unique to the phenomenographic approach. Again, as you may already know, as is the case for all research projects, one is required to be aware of and state biases and experiences. We will share how we arrived at and named our positionality, demonstrating and re-emphasising how interpretative awareness in research work is crucial. Drawing on examples from our own studies, and a range of others, we synthesise the different steps involved when planning such a research project.

In Chapter 4 we deal with data generation, which is core and common to qualitative research projects. Semi-structured interviews are the preferred method in phenomenographic work. We will cover this and introduce several other ways of generating data, including an overview of the often used 'spark' question or activity, designed to immerse participants in the experience of interest. Having the opportunity to see a range of practice methods in action will support readers to consider the approach most relevant and purposive for their research work.

Analysis and interpretation of said data forms Chapter 5. Again, there is no prescribed way of appraising the data; therefore, we will demonstrate how we each tackled this, paying attention to the tasks involved and to some of the other methods we have found to be useful and interesting from the literature. Phenomenography explicitly acknowledges the role of the researcher whose work it is to articulate how people report to perceive a phenomenon, through their descriptions of it. This goes to the core of what this research approach is all about.

Chapter 6 illustrates some of the ways of presenting findings. Phenomenographic results are usually reported in 'categories of description' and in so-called 'outcome spaces', and these too can take a variety of forms and formats. We again share versions from our work, to provide you with the context in which to examine ideas of how to graphically present study findings. In addition, we will offer examples from the wider body of phenomenographic literature, illustrating the creativity that often enriches the presentation of what was learnt from this type of research work.

The concluding chapter will look at the bigger and possible impacts of phenomenography. How and why people learn was and still is the *raison d'être* of phenomenography. We suggest ways in which these studies can help shape the education and research landscapes of today, and well into the future. Particularly in this time of uncertainty that increasingly involves artificial intelligence and large language models in learning, teaching and assessment in post-compulsory and higher education.

Throughout the book there are short 'pause and reflect' exercises to help readers review their learning. Each one is building on the last to support the development and consolidation of understandings. These learning pauses are also designed to help create your own phenomenographic project, which may take the form of postgraduate or indeed more substantial research. We recommend following the book in sequence, as each chapter is connected to the one before. But, of course, one can dip in and out of specific passages as is helpful.

It is worth pointing out that when completing the background reading for this book we were encouraged and refreshed by the work of fellow PhD student phenomenographers. Many have published their dissertations as monographs, and we will refer to some of them throughout this book. For future inspiration additional references and alternative ways of approaching this way of doing research are included. As noted by Åkerlind (2018: 956), 'we should not overlook the input of doctoral theses in maintaining creativity in a research field'. The resources section signposts to more information. Finally, we would like to stress that no book can replace the support one would get by engaging with an experienced phenomenographer. It is through this type of relational interaction, reflection and feedback that you would learn best 'how to do' this type of research. Nevertheless, we hope that our introductory guide provides a basic understanding of the steps involved and will inspire you to try out this most versatile research tool.

In addition, we include links to recommended further reading for each aspect of the approach, drawing from and on the work of a wide range of others, a sizeable percentage of whom form part of a robust and dynamic academic phenomenographic community, the European Association for Research on Learning and Instruction (EARLI 2023). They are colleagues who are deeply committed to the use and ongoing development of this approach.

2

Introducing phenomenography

In phenomenographic practice, the phenomenographer extracts descriptions of experience that are collated and presented through quotations. Ashwin (2005: 635) described how these *rich* or *thick* descriptions are selected to 'give some sense of the conception they are illustrating', because in phenomenographic work it can be 'unusual to find single quotations that perfectly illustrate each conception all of the time'. Fundamentally, phenomenography has a focus on human experience that is similar to that of, for example, naturalistic inquiry and grounded theory; however, it differentiates significantly in its application, and in how it functions to draw out structural and referential aspects of experience, and in its analysis, which is also different from the other interpretive research approaches (Cossham 2017).

As noted in Chapter 1, if you have already begun to read about phenomenography you may have found that much of the published literature involves terms and phrases that can appear or be experienced by the reader as confusing, or slightly contradictory. Which is why we advocate returning to the beginnings and early work of the founder and those that have progressed the approach, in a manner that is immersive. To absorb oneself in the early phenomenographic literature offers many advantages, alongside and in addition to building phenomenographic knowledge. Indeed, by journeying through the origins and developments and through engaging with the history one can be afforded with a real sense of authority, and an appreciation of becoming part of something quite rich, and quite special.

This introduction to phenomenography chapter offers an outline of its origins, the approach and how it was conceived of (Marton 1981). The chapter also situates and frames the key characteristics of phenomenography through examples from phenomenographic literature; in particular, those that demonstrate how and why the approach differs and where it diverges from other research approaches and methodologies. The prominent educationist Ference Marton is regarded as the founder of the concept for and within the educational context. His earlier (for example, Marton 1975; 1976; 1979; 1981; 1986; 1988) and persistent (for example, Marton 2015; 2018) contributions to it remain invaluable. Of particular significance is Marton's pivotal work 'Approaches to learning', coauthored with another accomplished phenomenographer, Roger Säljö (Marton and Säljö 1997). This chapter particularised the work that pre-empted and laid the foundations for phenomenography, as an approach to studying variation in people's experiences and in the realms of teaching, learning and student understanding.

Articulations building on Marton's work make clear, how, for phenomenographers, 'meaning is seen as being constituted in the relationship between the individual and the phenomenon' (Trigwell 2006: 369). Through the process of surfacing and analysing 'people's conceptions' (Svensson 1997: 160) phenomenographers can comment on and theorise about variations in experience. Excerpts from the work of other and established phenomenographers will be presented, including that of another of Marton's counterparts, Lennart Svensson, who has endowed the phenomenographic research community with a robust grounding in the history of the approach, including the early complexities, shifts, changes and challenges (Svensson 1997). The range of phenomenographic studies in circulation is expanding, including a selection of open access doctoral theses and dissertations. This brings a richness to the field of phenomenography through broadening the scope of creativity.

In situating the theoretical stance, Bruce (1999: 7–9), another admired and very well respected phenomenographer, has commented on and differentiated between the three descriptive research perspectives, 'the constructivist, the naturalistic, and the interpretative', for and within the phenomenographic context.

Bruce clarified how the interpretivist tradition is centred on the belief that different people experience the world differently, and the important point of how phenomenography is concerned with discovering these differences. In addition, while accurately placing phenomenography within the interpretative paradigm, together with phenomenology and hermeneutics, Bruce offered another significant observation, that, 'once the fundamental intentions of the phenomenographic research approach have been grasped, it is possible to implement studies at various levels of sophistication' (1999: 5).

As previously mentioned, through identifying how people interpret their experiences, phenomenographers can influence and shape understandings about the development, the construction and the encountering of an experience. Hence why we suggest the work and approaches of phenomenographers such as Åkerlind and Bruce should be embraced and embodied, because we have found them to induce the confidence necessary for developing ideas about what one can bring to the body of phenomenographic research knowledge. Associated with this literature familiarity is the need to pay attention to how phenomenography has grown in its relationship with variation theory (Ling and Marton 2012), and therefore where phenomenography is in its development (Marton 2015).

Historic developments

It is worth developing our earlier comment about how the origins of the term 'phenomenography' have been contested by Cibangu and Hepworth (2016: 151), who provided a rather convincing evidence trajectory. They traced the term back to Italian professor of mathematics Marco Tullio Falcomer, and before him, 'to a much earlier and more detailed use of the term by Swiss chemist Ludwig von Schmidt … in 1806'. They claim that the first recorded use by Falcomer was in 1902 (albeit as 'phénoménographie'), when he published an article in a French journal dealing with psychics. Within the phenomenographic community, it is still more widely believed that Ulrich Sonneman coined the term in 1954. While interesting, and perhaps even worth delving into further, including the work of Biggs (2003), the term is synonymous with the movement started and developed by Marton and colleagues at the University of Gothenburg in the 1970s. Cibangu and Hepworth (2016: 152) described this as 'Martonian phenomenography', building on from Marton's earlier 'approaches to learning' thinking (Biggs 2003: 5). Etymologically, the term 'phenomenography' is derived from the 'Greek phainomenon (appearance) and graphein (description), rendering phenomenography, a description of appearances' (Hasselgren and Beach 1997: 192). Different therefore, for example, from phenomenology, that seeks to 'study the phenomenon' directly, rather than studying how people are experiencing that phenomenon through their described experiences (Larsson and Holmström 2007: 62). It was initially this that Marton, and each and every phenomenographic researcher thereafter, aspired to: to seek, to surface, to describe and to impart ideas about the world as it appears to others.

The first recorded phenomenographic work began with the fundamental question, 'how shall we describe students' knowledge in the subjects taught and studied?' (Svensson 2016: 274). According to Pang (2003: 146) these initial studies tried to answer two specific questions: 'what does it mean, that some people are better at learning than others?' and 'why are some people better at learning than others?'. Marton and Säljö repudiated the conventional quantitative way of examining the outcomes of learning, which largely centre on the number of correct answers. They sought to understand deep learning, with a focus on *how* learning was being experienced rather than *what* students were learning. To test this, they devised an experiment:

> Two groups of 20 first-year students were asked to read three sections of a textbook. After the first two sections the groups received different types of questions. One group received questions which demanded a thorough understanding of the meaning of the passage. The other group was given detailed factual questions. After the concluding section of reading a common set of questions of both types was asked. Besides providing further evidence of qualitative differences in learning, the experiment showed that students did adapt their

way of learning to their conception of what was required of them. (Marton and Säljö 1976b: 15)

Dahlgren and Marton (1978: 25; italics in original) helpfully summarised these types of differences in understanding as 'learning is something that *happens* to you' versus 'learning is something that you *do*'. Pang (2003: 146) described this as the 'first face of variation', where studies concerned themselves with the question 'what are the different ways of experiencing the phenomenon?'. The outcome of these first studies resulted in the theory of 'deep' and 'surface' learning, which was appropriately stressed by Biggs (2003: 30) as relating to different approaches to learning, and not the 'characteristics of students'. Concepts that have stood the test of time, remaining central, or indeed should be, to the design of pedagogic practices today.

Interestingly, and related, is how Svensson (1977) analysed the same group of students as Marton and Säljö (as reported in Marton and Säljö 1976a and Marton and Säljö 1976b), going on to generate additional data by recalling the participants for two further sessions. In Svensson's work, students were asked what they had remembered about the text, and in addition, they were asked to read an extended version of this first text. Svensson took the view that knowledge and cognitive skill shared structures that were to be seen as unified, which he distinguished as 'atomistic' and 'holistic' cognitive approaches. The former was evident where students concentrated on 'specific comparisons, focusing on the parts of the text in sequence (rather than on the assumed more important parts), memorising details and direct information indicating a lack of orientation towards the message as a whole' (Svensson 1977: 238). This later approach showed an appreciation of the overall meaning that resulted in students 'searching for the author's intention, to relate the message to a wider context and/or to identify the main parts of the author's argument and supporting facts' (Svensson 1977: 238).

Since the initial work by Marton, and thereafter Marton and Säljö, many phenomenographic research studies have been designed and have reported on people's conceptions of a variety of phenomena. Ashwin et al (2015: 36) reported on how subsequent research into student learning across different countries, contexts and subject areas was remarkably stable and yielded the same broad categories of deep and surface. Elsewhere, researchers invested in investigating aspects of learning were also influenced by the deep and surface conceptualisation. Biggs (2003: 22), for example, and as referred to earlier, emphasised how the deep and surface learning conceptualisation 'generates strong implications for teaching', and how it shaped his approach to curriculum design, delivery, and assessment, namely 'constructive alignment'. According to Richardson (2015: 239), however, researchers often incorrectly cite these articles by Marton and Säljö as the source of the term 'phenomenography'. He argued that it was another paper by Marton (Marton 1976) which first introduced 'approach to learning' as a novel theoretical concept.

Over time, another form of phenomenography emerged owing to the work of Australian scholars who addressed different issues from the 'pure' version. Developmental phenomenography originated in applied research, due to how 'it seeks to find out how people experience some aspect of their world, and then to enable them or others to change the way their world operates, and it usually takes place in a formal educational setting' (Bowden 2000: 3). This emphasis on implications will resonate with researchers who need to justify their projects (see also Green and Bowden 2009). Based on Bowden's idea of phenomenographic pedagogy, this

> practical extension of the phenomenographic method worked on the simple idea that in any university classroom students will have, at most, five or six qualitatively different understandings of a subject or concept being taught. The challenge for the teacher is to come to terms with key aspects of these different ways of understanding, to explore the ways in which they differ and to work to help students to see the limitation of their existing perspectives. (Martin 2005: 288)

Topics subsequently investigated include, for example, 'researchers' conceptions of success in research' and 'ways of experiencing being a university teacher' (Bowden and Green 2005).

There have been other applications and focuses of the approach that are important to mention. Phenomenographic pedagogy provided the foundation to the 'approaches to teaching inventory', a widely used tool for appraising approaches to teaching in higher education (Trigwell et al 2005). Smith (2015), in her PhD dissertation which explored the phenomenon of political information, employed three theories: personal construct theory, phenomenography and critical pedagogical theory. Another doctoral thesis drew on a combination of social semiotics and phenomenography, when Patron (2022) investigated the role that visual representations play in the teaching and learning of chemistry, using the example of chemical bonding. Forster (2018) combined phenomenographic data derived from semi-structured interviews with additional ethnographic methods of data collection. Action research and phenomenography could complement each other as the students' experiences uttered in their own voices could lead to a changed curriculum based on the findings of action research (Beaulieu 2017).

Phenomenography has often been critiqued for having a messy and knotty relationship with phenomenology and its perceived ambiguity. Stolz (2020) claimed that phenomenography borrowed from phenomenology in a piecemeal fashion without applying the same rigour. However, contemporary phenomenological researchers were more robust in their analysis, with their commentary grounded in complementarity. Gibbs et al (1982) argued that phenomenology was about a methodology and phenomenography was substance-oriented. They had a deep appreciation of how phenomenography facilitated the ability to understand learning from the student's perspective, which can only add value to the design of in-text questions, other teaching devices and student-centric pedagogies. Uljens (1996) offered a phenomenographic self-reflection using a phenomenological lens.

Phenomenography has most certainly been influenced by phenomenology, given how each supports the investigation of human experience. As mentioned earlier, whereas phenomenology attempts to find the essence of phenomena (essentialist and foundationalist), phenomenography seeks to uncover variations in experience of phenomena (non-essentialist and non-foundationalist). Indeed, it overwhelmingly aims to describe phenomena 'through the variation of people's experience' (Limberg 2005: 281). The various categories of descriptions of these experiences, and the resulting relationships between these categories, form the so-called 'outcome space' (Limberg 2000). Phenomenological analysis, on the other hand, identifies 'meaning units' and emphasises individual experience, rather than collective meaning (Barnard et al 1999). Referring to the connection between both research specialisations, Marton and Booth (1997: 117) viewed phenomenography as a 'cousin-by-marriage' of phenomenology. Drawing on the strength of both, some researchers have combined phenomenographic and phenomenological analysis of data in their work (see, for example, Larsson and Holmström 2007). Ontologically, however, and what must be understood is that the approaches are significantly different. All of which we will deal with in greater detail, within each of the subsequent chapters.

The distribution of phenomenographic work happened organically and personal connections played a significant role in this, resulting in 'hot spots' of activities in certain countries, initially and predominantly in Sweden, with substantial research communities emerging latterly in Australia, the United Kingdom and Hong Kong. Pioneers in various locations and from within a variety of academic fields introduced the approach to their peers. For example, in information studies, Christine Bruce grounded her PhD work on information literacy using Marton. Bruce's (1997) seminal work on the discovery of seven conceptions, or 'faces' as she described them, of information literacy paved the way for many studies in this area. Halttunen (2003) adopted a phenomenographic approach in his investigation into students' conceptions of Information Retrieval (IR) and their perceptions of different skills needed for successful IR. Shenton and Hayter (2006) used phenomenography to investigate the term 'information' and library users' understandings of that term. Maybee (2006) took this approach to understand how undergraduate students conceptualised information use and expanded this in their PhD work to the relationship between a teacher and her students' experiences of information literacy in the classroom (Maybee 2015). In the United Kingdom, Boon et al (2007) conducted a phenomenographic study on the conceptions of information literacy among academics in English departments in universities. Andretta (2007) wrote a conceptual paper on how phenomenography could act as a framework for information literacy education. Young people's political information experiences were the focus of Smith and McMenemy's (2016) paper and Fázik and Steinerová (2021) researched new university students' experience of information literacy.

Learning and teaching in the professions also attracted several phenomenographic investigations, some of which are listed here. Dunkin (2000) researched organisational changes. 'Common sense' in workplace learning was investigated by Gerber (2001) and Collin (2006) conducted a study on design engineers' conceptions of workplace learning. Wheeler and McKinney (2015) used phenomenography to explore academic librarians' perceptions of their own teaching roles. Different professions are involved in the education of nurses and their conceptions of their own teaching and learning roles were investigated by Munangatire and McInerney (2022). Bruce and Stoodley (2013) probed the ways in which research supervision was seen as an exercise in teaching. In a more recent study, Lizier (2022) delved into the experiences of work and learning as described by professionals from a variety of industries in Sydney. These are just some examples of the kind of questions that benefited from the use of phenomenography. The relevance and rate of adoption of the approach has increased, and continues to increase, in a range of professional and scientific disciplines, including engineering, management, social work and medicine, among others.

The story of phenomenography does not end here! The turn of the century saw the appearance of 'variation theory', developed in Hong Kong (where Marton worked for several years). It was subsequently adopted in other countries, initially and predominantly in Sweden, making a full circle to where Marton devised phenomenography and later returned to. Variation theory originated in a desire to address and respond to some of the criticism of its perceived lack of theoretical stance. The method itself initially had a focus on learning studies, which aimed at understanding students' ways of sensemaking of the object of learning and which was built on the Japanese Lesson Study (Marton and Pang 2013). The main contribution of variation theory is 'that it brings the focus of the study sharply on the object of learning and provides a theoretical grounding to understand some of the necessary conditions for learning' (Ling and Marton 2012: 9). A typical example was a study by Lo (2012) where the researcher investigated whether applying variation theory could lead to improving teaching and learning in schools. Pang (2003: 146) called this the 'second face of variation' as it was not only concerned with the critical aspects of the phenomenon but also how the dimensions of variation were experienced by the person who discerned that variation. Rovio-Johansson and Ingerman, extremely well known for their work and their centrality to the phenomenographic community, usefully summarised the phenomenographic tradition in the following:

> [P]henomenography explores the qualitatively different ways in which people potentially 'experience' certain phenomena they meet in their worlds, variation theory offers a framework for understanding what it takes to experience something in a certain way (or learn about it), and learning studies make use of that framework to design teaching for good learning results. (Rovio-Johansson and Ingerman 2016: 261)

Åkerlind (2018) pointed out the commonalities of phenomenography and variation theory, which share the same theoretical framework including ontological and epistemological assumptions (discussed in detail further into this chapter). Pang and Ki (2016) distinguished between variation theory's analysis of naturalistic settings and learning studies' closeness to action research or design experiments. In practice, researchers often build on the findings of a phenomenographic study by applying a theoretical lens as afforded by variation theory. Forster (2016), for example, recommended this as a way of developing evidence-based interventions for information literacy education. Holmqvist and Selin (2019: 8) emphasised how combining both led to better understanding: phenomenography unveils how people understand a phenomenon and variation theory reveals how views can be developed by extracting the critical aspects.

The focus of this book, however, is on 'classic' or, in Marton's (1986) view, 'pure' phenomenography, given how our work looked at phenomena regarding course content and subsequent digital development and the acquisition of learning from everyday professional life, respectively. Namely, the contribution of social work education to the digital professionalism of students (Taylor-Beswick 2019) and the continuing professional development as understood by professional librarians (Hornung 2010). Within this, there is, of course, occasion to refer to variation theory, drawn from the seminal texts of Marton (2015) and Marton and Booth (1997), which demand a phenomenographer's attention. Most published studies on phenomenography can be found in academic journals, but there are also a handful of books written by experienced phenomenographers. We list them at the end of this book and would highly recommend usage so as to avoid that which Åkerlind (2022) pointed out, the many misunderstandings of phenomenography, its aims and procedures that often appear across the range of literatures.

Even though this remains a prolific research community, from the very beginning there was surprisingly little published work in terms of theory. Two texts which brought together assumptions and theoretical thinking were not published until the 1990s: Marton and Booth's 'Learning and awareness' in 1997 and Bowden and Marton's 'University of learning' in 1998 (reprinted in 2004). As Marton himself acknowledged, and earlier in this work, early phenomenographic research was met with criticism regarding its assumptions and methodology, and therefore rightly forced the pioneers to state its basic epistemological principles (Marton 1988). Critics suggested a reworking of phenomenography in a constructionist fashion (Richardson 1999) or using phenomenological underpinnings (Hasselgren and Beach 1997). Some years later, two edited volumes dealing with methods that became points of reference for students in particular, Bowden and Walsh (2000) and Bowden and Green (2005), followed. This lack of agreed terminology and practical guidance has led to real difficulties for the research community. Richardson (2015: 256) pointedly claimed that Svensson (1977), who had been an early collaborator of Marton and Säljö, confused terms when he 'used the approach to refer to the students' activities during the experimental sessions and during their academic studies and not to refer to their underlying attitudes or dispositions to learning'.

Looking at the available literature, a considerable amount of variation can still be detected. Authors, out of the need to not repeat themselves, use many terms interchangeably, but in doing so run the risk of confusing matters further. For the novel researcher, this can be perplexing and overwhelming. This is something that is dealt with in the next and subsequent chapters.

Key aspects of phenomenography

Fundamentally, phenomenography has one single phenomenon as the object of study, underpinned by two generic and overarching questions: 'what is learned?' and 'how is it learned?' (Kullberg and Ingerman 2022: np). Among the first phenomenographic investigations was a study designed to generate students' understanding of basic concepts in microeconomics (Dahlgren and Marton 1978). As noted, since then, there has been a rich and varied collection of topics examined by researchers. We argue that any phenomenon would lend itself to being examined through a phenomenographic lens and we invite you to contribute to the ever-expanding literature with studies of new and previously unreported phenomena. To provide a further flavour of conventional areas of investigations, it is useful to refer to a recent article by Åkerlind (2022: 3), who cited examples of phenomena of study, drawn from the early work of Marton and Booth (1997):

- Learning (amongst young students in one study and amongst university students in another)
- Numbers (amongst young children)
- Recursion (amongst computer programming students)
- Newtonian motion (amongst physics students)
- Matter (amongst chemistry students)
- Political power (amongst members of a community).

Some of these might resonate, or readers may well have an equally distinct area of interest arising from their background, experiences and, perhaps, priorities in their profession. At an early stage in your research journey and/or any form of doctoral study, it is prudent to be clear in the identification of a phenomenon central to the work. In terms of next steps, this involves thinking out of the philosophical implications, those that will form the basis of a thesis.

As outlined previously, novice phenomenographers can be somewhat overwhelmed by some seemingly confusing statements and terminology, hindered further by the development of the approach and how it was applied across different countries and jurisdictions, involving researchers speaking and writing in different languages. It appears that, occasionally, translations miss the nuances of the researchers' meaning when they report on their findings. Nevertheless, there is agreement on the following distinct features which define phenomenography:

- It is non-dualistic in its ontology and epistemology
- It is about the structure of human awareness
- It is about the dialectical relationship between meaning and structure
- Phenomenographic interviews are open ended and use probing questions. (Åkerlind 2022: 1)

The following part of this chapter will elaborate on each of these points, because of how fundamental this is to the development understanding of this research approach, and the need to articulate and apply them robustly within a written dissertation or research report, and where relevant, the viva examination. Similar to any other qualitative work, it is crucial to reflect on one's beliefs about the world and the place these beliefs may have on one's grasp and previous knowledge of the phenomenon under investigation. All these positions impact on the researcher's stance. Thus, there is a need for explicitness when writing up a phenomenographic research study to provide convincing and accessible arguments. Needless to say, we hope that your understandings of reality and knowledge are in line and coalesce with phenomenographic standpoints!

In foregrounding essential theoretical positions, every research paradigm, every basic belief system has underlying ontological and epistemological questions. They are 'what is there that can be known/what is the nature of reality?', also known as your 'ontological question', and 'what is the relationship of the knower to the known?', or epistemological question (Guba and Lincoln 1989: 83). Both the ontological and epistemological stances in phenomenography are non-dualistic. This means that there is no division between an outer and an inner world, but that there is only one world, the one we experience (Marton and Booth 1997; Bowden 2005a). The epistemological assumption in phenomenography is one of 'intentionality', which states that 'knowledge is intentionally constituted through individuals' conceptions of reality' (Sandberg 1996: 135). This is a view that it shares with phenomenology. The differences in experience one person has can be described and understood by other people (Sjöström and Dahlgren 2002). This approach contrasts with dualistic epistemologies, for example, the positivist/objectivist view (external reality exists) or the cognitivist/constructivist view (individuals' internal constructions are the focus) (Åkerlind 2015). In fact, phenomenography is completely unconcerned with the nature of reality, it takes a second-order perspective, hence why it is commensurate with a host of learning theories.

In phenomenography, the focus is on this 'second-order perspective' and the objects of research are the 'underlying ways of experiencing the world, phenomena, and situations' (Marton and Booth 1997: 118) by human beings. This research can be done in two ways. Marton and Neuman (1996: 317) elaborated on how an experience, a conception, is formed as the result of the relationship between a person ('subject', a term which is not used any more) and an object. If the aim of the study is how the individual perceives of something in relation to how others do (which means we are looking for variation between individuals), the focus is on the object aspect. If, however, the goal is to compare the person's way of understanding something to how they experience other things, the focal point is the person themselves. Viewed from this alternative angle, the researcher's role has many different layers: 'it means taking the place of the respondent, trying to see the phenomenon and the situation through her eyes, and living her experience vicariously' (Marton and Booth 1997: 121). More importantly, the researcher needs to bracket their own insights and expertise, limiting it to instances where further explanation of the respondent's utterances was needed. This is a key skill a phenomenographic researcher needs to develop and one that doctoral students tend to struggle with. Dringenberg et al (2015) reflected on how they negotiated this challenge in their respective doctoral projects and offered some advice: careful listening without judgement; being open to new ideas; using follow-up questions mindfully; and reflecting on one's own understanding of what the person had said. Marton and Booth (1997: 108) emphasised that the structure of a person's awareness is fluid, evolving and changing all the time: 'if awareness is the totality of all experiences, then awareness is as descriptive of the world as it is of the person'.

The basic unit of description in phenomenographic research is a 'conception', which 'has been called various names, such as "ways of conceptualising", "ways of experiencing", "ways of seeing", "ways of apprehending", "ways of understanding", and so on' (Marton and Pong 2005: 336). Many researchers have moved away from using the term 'conception' due to how it had been used in psychology to denote cognitive activity. It is useful, however, to peruse all these terms interchangeably to reduce any possibility of misinterpretation. Phenomenography groups conceptions into categories of descriptions, which will manifest themselves across different situations, and therefore form 'a kind of collective intellect' (Marton 1981: 177). These categories are limited in number and internally related (Trigwell 2006). The result of phenomenographic research is then presented in what is termed an 'outcome space', which shows the similarities and differences between categories of descriptions and is usually, but not always, found to be hierarchical in nature. It follows that the focus during data analysis is not on the individual, who may hold different views about one single phenomenon, but rather on the differences between conceptions of phenomena (Limberg 1999). The aim is 'to explore the range of meanings within a sample group, as a group, not the range of meanings for each individual within the group' (Åkerlind 2005d: 323). It is essential to stress that one individual can hold more than one conception depending on the situation and the question asked (Marton and Pong 2005).

A conception consists of two parts which are 'dialectically intertwined aspects' (Marton and Pong 2005). Rather confusingly, however, over time terminology changed as phenomenographers developed two frameworks to aid with analysing these conceptions. Initially, researchers used 'how/what' distinctions (not to be confused with the generic research questions of 'how and what is learned' mentioned earlier), with 'referential/ structural' differentiations added later. As Harris (2011) noted in a review of phenomenographic studies, there were anomalies and inconsistencies in usage throughout. According to Marton and Booth (1997: 91) where 'learning' was the subject of investigation, the 'what (direct object of learning)/how (the indirect object of learning and the act of learning)' model applied, whereas 'experience' could be described in terms of referential aspect (meaning) and structural aspect (structure), with its internal and external horizons. 'While capturing the meaning of a concept is a matter of interpreting what a person is saying, the structural aspect can be identified by linguistic markers' (Marton and Pong 2005: 345). Marton and Booth used the image of a deer against the backdrop of a dark forest to explain the internal and external horizons:

> Thus, the external horizon of coming on the deer in the woods extends from the immediate boundary of the experience – the dark forest against which the deer is discerned – through all other contexts in which related occurrences have been experienced (for example walks in the forest, deer in the zoo, nursery tales, reports of hunting incidents, etc.). The internal horizon comprises the deer itself, its parts, its stance, its structural presence. (Marton and Booth 1997: 87)

Marton and Booth (1997) combined both frameworks in their diagram on the experience of learning, which is, of course, the focus of variation theory (see Figure 2.1).

Ultimately, these aspects support the analysis of data. Examples outlined in Chapter 6 (see Figures 6.1, 6.3 and 6.4) will illustrate how we and others have employed these terms and methods, and in addition what helped us with sensemaking.

Underlying the conceptions are 'dimensions of variation'. These 'themes running across the data are called dimensions

Introducing phenomenography

Figure 2.1: The experience of learning

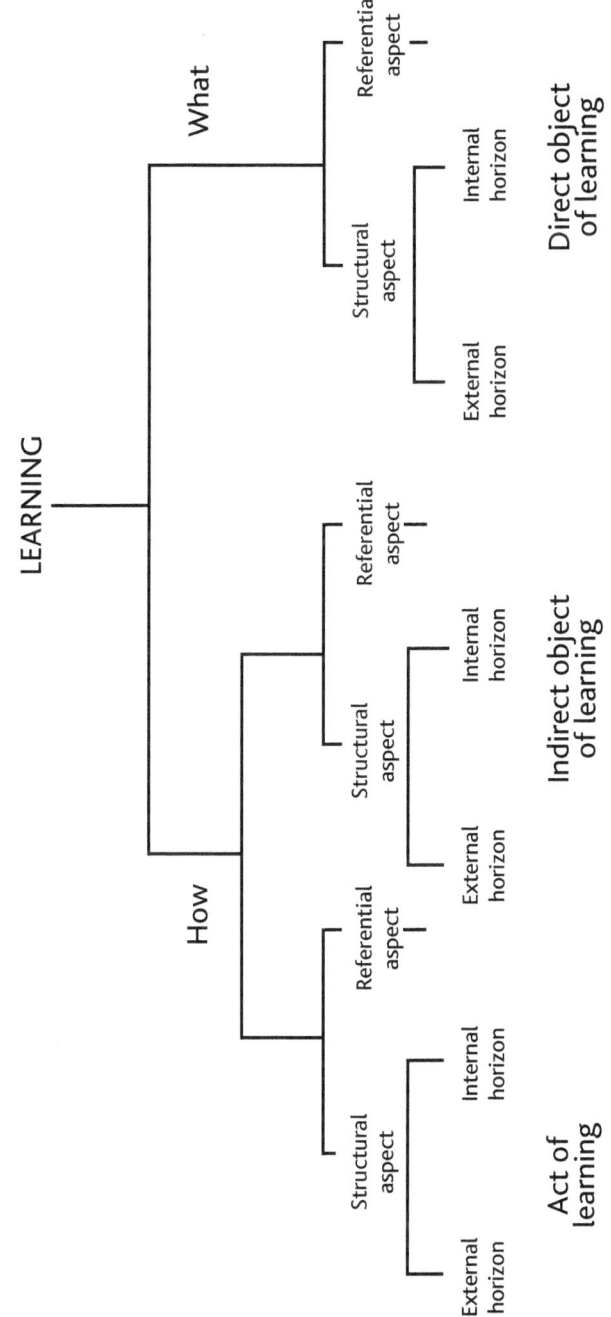

Source: Marton and Booth (1997: 91)

of variation, because they reveal the aspects differentiating the categories' (Kettunen and Tynjälä 2018: 6). Stoodley et al (2018: 405) emphasised how 'the dimensions operate across all categories and no one dimension is associated with any one category'. These are crucial elements in phenomenography and for phenomenographers.

> In order for learning to take place, the learner has to discern a critical aspect or dimension of variation in the phenomenon; she has to see how this aspect can vary; and she has to become simultaneously aware of the possible 'values' [inverted commas in the original] along this dimension of variation in order to compare them. (Dahlin 2007: 328)

Marton and Pang (2006) use the example of colour, pointing out that a person would not be able to perceive the colour of things if there was only one colour. In summary, dimensions of variation are 'aspects of the individual's experience of something' (Marton and Booth 1997: 209).

As was the case with conceptions as noted earlier, different researchers apply different terminology, and not always consistently. Bowden et al (2005: 139) employed the term 'themes of expanding awareness', 'because the alternative "dimension of variation" is now used ambiguously in the literature'. A lack of definition in early theoretical work can, and often is, blamed for the confusion. According to Pang and Ki this concept had been used in different ways:

- In traditional phenomenographic research, it serves as a pragmatic tool to structure and arrange the outcome space;
- In variation theory, it is more theoretically grounded and regarded as a synonym to 'dimension of variation' with critical features being the target values;
- In a learning study, it is an aspect that is critical to a learner's acquirement of the object of learning. (Pang and Ki 2016: 324)

Perhaps not surprisingly, there are also different ways of presenting the outcome space. It may be a linear model (one more sophisticated than the one before), but it could also take the form of branching structures or hierarchies showing an inclusiveness of categories (Åkerlind 2005d). Additionally, researchers have come up with different ways of visually representing the outcome space. Chapter 6 is where we will deal with these issues.

Pause and reflect exercise

1. Invest time thinking about your own philosophical outlook and your views on qualitative and quantitative research.

2. Outline your initial views on phenomenography and how it might apply in your subject area, practice or discipline.

3. What might be your next steps?

3

Research design and ethics in phenomenographic work

This chapter will highlight some of the decisions and choices involved in the design of a phenomenographic study, which will lead to a robust articulation of the rationale for using the approach. Coming to appreciate that there are many ways of structuring and carrying out a piece of phenomenographic research is integral to becoming a phenomenographer. We will also pay attention to ethical considerations. Straub and Maynes (2021: 73) described how the design of phenomenographic work is 'predicated on the rigorous process by which the researcher undertakes a careful plan for achieving a particular goal'. As Entwistle (1997: 128), however, made clear, 'some qualitative research, claiming to be phenomenographic, has been conducted without the necessary rigour, either in design or analysis'. This is something to be avoided. Thus, paying attention to and dealing with each key and discrete aspect of the study design must be given centrality and will be the focus of this chapter. We will deal with data generation, transcription, analysis, and reporting and dissemination more fully in Chapters 4–6. In working through each aspect of the study design we will again offer a range of perspectives. Perspectives we began sharing in Chapter 1, that described how phenomenographic work 'involves the interpretation of descriptions of experiences of a phenomenon' (Forster 2016: 353) to capture variation in the way it is experienced (Åkerlind 2005d; 2018). Again, we will refer to and offer examples from our doctoral work and provide examples from other published phenomenographic studies, those that offer design clarity, including, where relevant, the work from the rich tapestry of studies offered by PhD students.

Designing phenomenographic work

As noted, there are a number of component parts in the design and structuring of a phenomenographic research project. As alluded to in Chapter 1, what many others (some almost 20 years earlier) continue to point out is a distinct lack of guidance or insufficient guidance within the phenomenographic research literature; that which is necessary to gaining the understandings and skills fundamental for doing phenomenographic work. To grasp the practicalities involved in conducting such a study, one has to read far beyond what would be thought of as normal or expected when reading for research work. An issue that often results in wrestling and grappling with understandings, and that drives the angst that we have previously mentioned, is associated with *how to do* phenomenographic work, *how to do it well* and *how to do it right* (Åkerlind 2005a; Alsop and Tompsett 2006). The dearth of procedural resources continues to present, more recently in the writings of Straub and Maynes (2021: 74), who felt compelled to make an attempt at rectifying the situation by introducing a model they explain as being 'adapted from phenomenography literature'. The model involves a useful 15-step process, which they classify in 'linear' and 'recursive' stages, that combines the more general sequence of design with the iterative analytical work that flows from it. This visual representation (Figure 3.1) of their model provides a practical capture of phenomenographic methodology, a valuable accompaniment to textual explanations that can be used to strengthen the development of phenomenographic skills and understandings.

There are a variety of other design methods and approaches found across the breadth of phenomenographic literatures, with the following practical outline developed by Ashworth and Lucas (2000) proving to be particularly popular (Box 3.1). Interestingly, Ashworth and Lucas (2000: 298) offered a similar rationale to that of Straub and Maynes (2021: 73) for what prompted them to develop this study design outline, citing the 'need to clarify

Figure 3.1: Phenomenography methodology

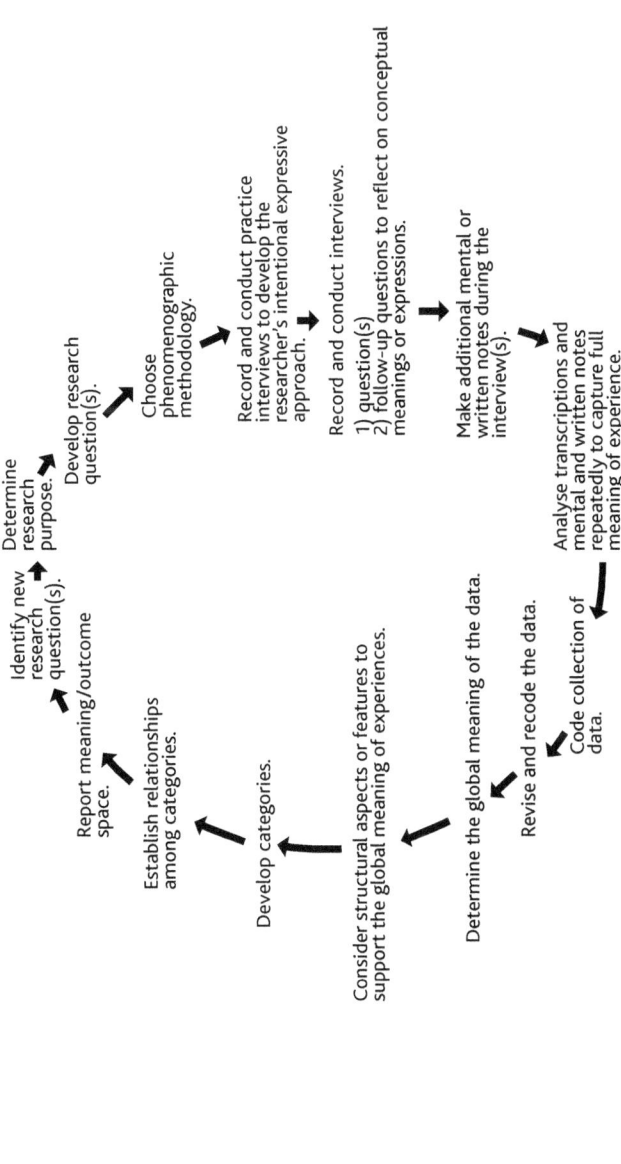

Source: Straub and Maynes (2021: 74)

important aspects of the methodology so that it can be used with increasing effectiveness'.

Box 3.1: Practical guidelines for the conduct of phenomenographic research

1. The researcher should tentatively identify the broad objectives of the research study, the phenomenon under investigation, recognising the meaning of this area may be quite different for the research participant.
2. The selection of the participants should avoid presuppositions about the nature of the phenomenon, or the nature of conceptions held by particular 'types' of individual while observing common-sense precautions about maintaining 'variety' of experience.
3. The most appropriate means of obtaining an account should be identified, allowing maximum freedom for the research participant to describe their experience.
4. In obtaining experiential accounts the participant should be given the maximum opportunity to reflect, and the questions posed should not be based on researcher presumptions about the phenomenon or the participant but should emerge out of the interest to make clear *their* experience.
5. The researcher's interviewing skills should be subject to an ongoing review and changes made to interview practice if necessary. For instance, stylistic traits which tend to foreclose description should be minimised.
6. The transcription of the interview should be aimed at accurately reflecting the emotions and emphases of the participant.
7. The analysis should continue to be aware of the importation of presuppositions and be carried out with the maximum exercise of empathic understanding.
8. Analysis should avoid premature closure for the sake of producing logically and hierarchically related categories of description.
9. The process of analysis should be sufficiently clearly described to allow the reader to evaluate the attempt to achieve bracketing and empathy and trace the process by which findings have emerged.

Source: Ashworth and Lucas (2000: 30; italics in original)

As previously noted, for the writing of this work we each revisited our doctoral theses and subsequent publications (Hornung 2010; 2012; Taylor 2017; Taylor-Beswick 2019; 2023), and relating to this section, as a reminder of how we had constructed our research questions and project titles, and how we designed and articulated the rationale for our respective studies. In terms of design and study articulation, Box 3.2 illustrates how the step-by-step guideline by Ashworth and Lucas influenced the design approach taken in the phenomenographic study on librarians' professional development (Hornung 2010).

Box 3.2: Phenomenographic study design in a doctoral thesis

1. The researcher introduced the project to each interviewee using the same opening statement highlighting the aim of the study.
2. The call for participants was advertised widely, thus allowing interested parties to partake without any pre-selection on part of the researcher resulting in a huge variety.
3. Semi-structured interviews were chosen to elicit responses.
4. The researcher aimed at giving participants time to reflect on their experiences. Follow-up questions were used to clarify statements.
5. The pilot study revealed some shortcomings with the interview technique, eg speed of speech and asking leading questions. The researcher reflected on this and discussed it with the supervisor. She also revised her skills after each interview by writing down her impressions on how it went. Furthermore, she started transcribing almost immediately after each interview, which in turn helped inform her interviewing skills.
6. The researcher transcribed all interviews verbatim. This included recording words that were emphasised by the interviewee by highlighting them. She also noted obvious emotions, such as being uncomfortable with a question resulting in evasive answers. Each transcript was read and re-read several times constantly checking for accuracy.
7. Each interview underwent several cycles of analysis both on an individual basis and as part of the whole dataset. Each statement was read several times – on its own and in the context of surrounding sentences to ensure that the researcher understood the respondent.
8. The researcher exercised great care during analysis not to draw any conclusions before she had finished examining all transcripts. At several

points she stopped to check on emerging themes, which were then grouped and re-grouped. This went on throughout the analytical process as more transcripts were being added. Only after the final interview had been cut up did she try to define these categories of description. During several meetings with the supervisor these categories were debated.
9. The researcher documented all steps taken by taking photographs and kept a log of the emerging categories and dimensions as they presented themselves.

Source: Hornung (2010: 126–127)

As would be expected in the world of qualitative research work, not all phenomenographers take the same approach to study design or study design articulation, with most offering a rationale for the study approach at the outset along with design decisions and choices largely woven throughout the text. Within the context of doctoral work there is an expectation that content of this nature will be sufficiently elaborated and expanded upon within the initial project proposal, typically and particularly as part of the methodology section of the work (Box 3.3).

Box 3.3: Phenomenographic study rationale in a doctoral thesis

The design of this study was influenced by how preparedness in social work education is conceptualised, anxieties about how preparedness can realistically be facilitated and an optimism about what, in relation to digital preparedness, through this research, can be learnt. This chapter deals with the methodology, the methods and the means used to cogenerate data that would reveal students' perspectives on their digital experiences in social work education. Insights that would allow for an examination of the contribution of social work education to the digital professionalism of students in preparation for practice in the connected age. This chapter outlines phenomenography and its relevance as an approach through which to understand more about how social work education prepares social work students to practice in a world that increasingly includes digital aspects. It draws heavily on the work of phenomenographers, those who are well established in its application and those who have contributed substantially to its development as a research approach in the education field. It begins by outlining the philosophical stance which shaped the methodological decisions that were made. It provides further rationale for why this study is needed, and for why it is needed now. As noted in the prologue 'every inquiry is guided beforehand by what is sought' (Heidegger, 1962, p. 24). The purpose of a research study therefore determines the methodological choice. Given that the focus of this study is human experience an interpretative approach was the most appropriate approach through which to access relevant thought. In this study human experience relates to:

1. Social work students' experiences of digital development, throughout the duration of their professional training
2. How digital development was perceived to have been facilitated, or how conceptions of digital professionalism were formed,

as described by students, or from the student point of view. In contrast to positivists, interpretivists seek to better understand 'the social life world' (Crotty, 1998, p. 67). They believe that phenomena can only be understood through accessing the meanings people attribute to it. The fact that meanings are subjective, suggests that they are also variable; a point that underpins the phenomenographic approach. It is this variability that phenomenographers seek to surface.

Source: Taylor-Beswick (2019: 48–49)

Similar to other qualitative research design, phenomenographic research should include an 'overall strategy and rationale; site/ population selection and sampling; the researcher's role and ethics; data collection methods; data management; data analysis strategy; trustworthiness; and a timeline' (Marshall and Rossman 2016: 99).

Research question

In thinking about the construction of the research question or questions, it is essential to deliberate the overall intention, the purpose of the work, and to interrogate all of the aforementioned in an appropriate amount of detail. There are various means to accessing feedback on your initial ideas, one of which is to ask yourself a number of key questions, to ensure that the study design is necessary, clear, focused and aligned to the study intentions. The following are examples of the kinds of trigger questions relevant to supporting the identification and development of the research focus:

- What is the purpose of my research?
- What am I seeking to explore, describe, analyse?
- Is my research question relevant and significant?
- Have I engaged fully with relevant literature?
- Is my research question original?
- Is my research question specific?
- Can my research question be answered?
- Is my research question clear and unambiguous?
- Does my research question align with the phenomenographic approach?

It is important to note that different research methods aims dictate what kind of questions can be investigated. For example, in ethnographic research the focus is on the analysis of people's behaviour in a particular context, whereas grounded theory examines social processes and meaning leading to theory building. Phenomenology investigates people's lived experience of a phenomenon, in direct contrast therefore with phenomenography, which is interested in the variation in ways of experiencing.

It is also important to define, but not confuse, the research questions with the research project title. The project title should consist of a concise, descriptive phrase that provides an overview of the study. It ideally should capture the essence of the research, be informative and indicative of the main focus or objective of the research and include keywords or key concepts related to the research topic.

Sampling

At the heart of a phenomenographic research project are human beings, human relationships, an object of study and the researcher's interpretation of the same. Interactions occur within a research field and involve a smallish group of people, who have experience of a specific phenomenon, at a particular moment in time, and within a particular context. Similar to other qualitative research approaches, target population and selection decisions are essential to the coherence and robustness of a study design, given how they will ultimately shape the course that one will take, the results that are surfaced and the manner in which these are reported on. Yet, and again, there is limited discussion about sampling and sampling methods within phenomenographic literatures, and 'what has been written evidences differences in opinion relating to sampling methods and sample size' (Trem 2017 in Taylor-Beswick 2019: 58).

The number of people needed for a viable study remains deeply contested, with the volume of participants varying significantly across phenomenographic projects. Experienced phenomenographers recommend 15 to 20 participants, deeming that fewer than 10 to 15 is too little to investigate variation fully, and more than 20 to create too much data (researcher interviewed in Trigwell 2000). Bowden (2005a) outlined that most phenomenographers use between 20 and 30 interviews. Davis (2007: 146) commended a 'kind of controlled bias' in the sample group, with the range of people big enough to explore different and comparative experiences and with participants who will have views different to that of the researcher. This is often referred to in the literature as 'saturation'. Åkerlind (2007: 242), unsurprisingly, given the pragmatic wisdom that she brings to the field, advised phenomenographic researchers 'to aim for the minimum sample that can be expected to show the range of variation that would be present in the population as a whole'. For a slightly longer and comparative discussion on sampling see Taylor-Beswick (2019: 58–62).

Regardless, the first decision that must be made when embarking upon phenomenographic work is consideration of the population relevant to the study, who to recruit and where to recruit from. It is worth pointing out that there are logistical and ethical aspects to this decision and matters that clearly will be dictated by the overall purpose of the research work. Here we offer some trigger questions designed to support the interrogation of the participant sampling process, those that we have found fundamental to making robust sampling decisions:

- Age cohort: bearing in mind that research with children, for example, requires parental/school consent procedures and additional measures to protect participants during and after the study.
- Vulnerability: people with disabilities, for example, might need support personnel or technical aids during and after the study; securing consent might be more complex and require thought to how inclusion is facilitated and to how the right to involvement is maintained.
- Availability: if you are engaging in a research project bound by time limits, it is important to consider if participants have been made aware of the time commitments and restrictions, and can be enlisted for the period required to have a valid study and sample.
- Experience: it is crucial that participants have a reasonable amount of experience of the object of study. Remember, participants will need to be able to articulate their views about the same phenomenon, and it is the researcher's responsibility to facilitate articulation.

Having established these and other study-specific parameters, the next step is to recruit participants. If investigating a phenomenon outside a specific environment (for example, a cohort of students in a classroom, which is by its nature self-limiting), consideration must be given to what is a relatively regular feature of phenomenographic studies, purposive sampling. Essentially, the selection is based on judgement, as to who will have had experience in the specific topic (Robson 1993: 141). This sampling method is widely used in phenomenographic research due to the emphasis on maximising variation in ways of experiencing a phenomenon, which requires a broad variation of characteristics of the participants (see, for example, Limberg 2000; Green 2005). Collier-Reed and Ingerman (2013: 250) argued that this type of sampling allows for participants to be selected as 'critical cases', based on who is most likely to provide variation in experience.

Another method worth considering is a specific form of purposive sampling, 'a priori criteria sampling', mainly because of how it prompts the establishment of a sampling framework

(Hornung 2010: 139). This sampling technique allows the researcher to draw up criteria that could influence participants' experiences, such as gender, location or work setting, which will be identified through the literature review. Next is the development of a grid outlining these relationships. Grid cells are subsequently populated with names of individuals using more inductive type methods (Pickard 2007). This method corresponds with maximum variation sampling, which actively helps the researcher identify diverse characteristics in the sample, for example, geographical variation, age, gender, stage in career and so on, and picks participants who are as different as possible (Patton 2002).

Ethics

With regards to matters of ethics when engaged in phenomenographic work, considerations are similar to ethical considerations in any research work involving human actors (for example, Wiles 2013; Barrow et al 2022). Kara (2018) characterised a set of ethical principles in circulation that researchers can draw on: largely discipline, institution, funder and jurisdiction orientated. We strongly suggest a review of Kara's publication, given how it immerses the reader in a wide range of ethics literature, ethical potentialities and ethical challenges. Regardless of the ethical guidance a researcher is required to adhere to, there are a number of generic principles found in most research literature, such as the commitment to avoid or minimise harm, uphold rights, protect privacies, ensure consent is clear and secured, and that participation is entirely on a voluntary basis.

Expanding on these universal conventions, Brinkmann and Kvale (2015), in their book designed to prepare researchers for interview practice, outlined the ethical issues, as pertaining to crucial stages of the research project (see Box 3.4).

Box 3.4: Ethical issues at seven research stages

Thematising. The purpose of an interview study should, beyond the scientific value of the knowledge sought, be considered with regard to improvement of the human situation investigated.

Designing. Ethical issues of design involve obtaining the subjects' [*sic*] informed consent to participate in the study, securing confidentiality, and considering the possible consequences for the study of the subjects [*sic*].

Interview situation. The personal consequences of the interview interaction for the subjects [*sic*] needs to be taken into account, such as stress during the interview and changes in self-understanding.

Transcription. The confidentiality of the interviewees needs to be protected, and there is also the question of whether a transcribed text is loyal to the interviewee's oral statements.

Analysis. Ethical issues in analysis involve the question of how penetratingly the interviews can be analysed and of whether the subjects [*sic*] should have a say in how their statements are interpreted.

Verification. It is the researcher's ethical responsibility to report knowledge that is as secured and verified as possible. This involves the issue of how critically an interviewee may be questioned.

Reporting. There is again the issue of confidentiality when reporting private interviews in public and of the consequences of the published report for the interviewees and for the groups they belong to.

Source: Brinkmann and Kvale (2015: 85–86; italics in original)

When designing a research project, ethical approval is normally required. Therefore, the researcher will need to convince an ethics committee that potential participants' wellbeing, the research environment, and the use and storage of data have been rigorously considered. Interviewees, of course, have the right to an honest representation of their voice in the interview and to have access to the raw data. Member checking can add validity to the data because the researcher engages in an ongoing dialogue with the participant throughout the analysis process (Cresswell and Cresswell 2018: 208). Unlike other qualitative approaches, member checking is not widely practised in phenomenography, given how the first stage of data analysis involves a pooling of meanings from across all of the transcripts, an integral and intricate part of forming the categories of description (Green 2005: 44). Additional problems can arise where individuals wish to view a transcript of their recording. In phenomenography this can be a particularly complex issue, in circumstances where the researcher has already applied some interpretation to the primary data, in forms of highlighting pauses and pronunciation and some preliminary coding (Oliver 2003). An example of how this can be dealt with is available in the previously mentioned doctoral work on librarians' professional development (Hornung 2010). In this instance, each participant was offered a copy of their recording and information about how to access the final report. Interestingly, only two of 30 interviewees took up the offer, with one seeking clarifications on certain utterances, which then were cross-checked with the real-time recording. The researcher listened to the recording again and found the transcript to be a true account of what had been said. On further contact the interviewee agreed this to be the case.

Another ethical challenge that can occur is when participants have difficulties expressing their views and opinions or where their form of expression is different from that of the researchers. As Hallett (2014) pointed out, phenomenography relies heavily on semi-structured interviews and this could exclude some people, such as those with additional learning needs or communication difficulties. Therefore, when designing the interview strategy, accommodations should be made for participants' communication needs and choices. This should be the dominant consideration, not that which is deemed to be common practice or that which is convenient.

Interview strategy

It is important to keep in mind when designing a phenomenographic study the need to make sure that 'all participants are commenting on the same phenomenon, not of different (even if related) phenomena' (Åkerlind 2022: 2). This is a core requirement in phenomenographic work and one of the reasons why it is worthwhile to conduct pilot interviews before embarking on a full and thorough phenomenographic project. Go and Pang

(2021) reflected on how ignoring the importance of focusing on a single common context compromised their data collected. The participants in their pilot study shifted their attention to other related but personal circumstances and the researcher had failed to draw their attention back to interview scenarios developed to frame the context. While the semi-structured interview was historically the preferred method of data generation, the nuances of what constitutes communication, semi-structured or otherwise, requires an appropriate amount of attention. Associated with this is how one captures and maintains participant focus on the phenomenon of interest. We will address this in detail in the data generation section.

Positionality

Recognising one's positionality is central to conducting good social research; an issue influenced by a researcher's values, worldview and background. Holmes (2020) advised that novice researchers should reflect on these factors, bearing in mind that positionality is fluid and can change over time and in different contexts. The positionality of participants is also relevant, as Piedra (2023) discovered, given the immense variation in how people experience – and are willing to articulate – their position in life. If the researcher accepts the stance of participants and can harness this through meaningful interactions during interviews, deeply rich situated knowledge can be brought to the surface. This 'intentional-expressive' approach of interviewing in phenomenography promotes reflection in participants and requires the researcher to encourage people to explore and clarify what has been said and gently probe where statements or utterances seem unclear or appear partial (Sin 2010: 310).

Other factors requiring consideration are the motivations of participants and the situational dynamics, both the actual and the potential, including those that will exist between researcher and participant. One of the key principles of interviewing is to make sure that researchers respect interviewees by conducting the study in a way that supports or enhances their dignity (Seidman 2013: 143). Regarding insider–outsiderness, Holmes suggested that often these lines are blurred and that 'the social-historical-political location of a researcher influences their orientations, i.e., that they are not separate from the social processes they study' (Holmes 2020: 3). Kara (2012: 11) advised that attention is paid to the nuances of the 'insider-researcher' conceptualisation and to how 'identities' can and do 'overlap and interact' within the research environment. For Thomas (2009: 147), what must be acknowledged is 'what is right for researcher might not be right for the participant'. Naming and navigating tensions forms part of robust ethical research practice.

Robustness of the design

Demonstrating research integrity is vital, so that colleagues, stakeholders and various publics can have confidence in the approach taken and the accuracy of the findings (Israel and Hay 2006: 5). Traditionally, the researcher attended to the trustworthiness of the research design by addressing the validity and reliability of the data generated and interpretations of the same. These terms originated in quantitative research, and it is important to notice that in qualitative research, which often entails small-scale research projects, they take on a slightly different hue. We will outline in the following sections how phenomenographers handle these criteria by drawing on established principles and showing how they have applied them in some of their publications.

Trustworthiness

The criterion of trustworthiness is guided by context and evidenced by the decisions, choices and steps taken throughout the research process. Explicitness is crucial at each of the different stages of a study. Collier-Reed et al (2009) distinguished between three domains of the research project: the domain of the researcher; that of the collective; and that of the individual participant. The researcher's domain implies a general awareness of one's own role in, and motivation for, conducting this project as well as its purpose. Holmes (2020) added that one's positionality influenced what is believed to be true and valid in other people's research. The domain of the collective concerns itself with the outcome of a phenomenographic study, namely a set of categories that show the possible ways in which all participants were represented, capturing the knowledge on a collective level. Lastly, the level of the individual requires paying attention to the individual's context as experienced and what they are focusing on (for a more detailed description see Collier-Reed et al 2009).

A refreshing example of robust reflexivity and explicitness in action is found in the work of Go and Pang (2021), who offered reflections on how a pilot study they conducted took an unexpected turn, illuminating their need to become more established in phenomenographic practices. Issues included a lack of control of the interview situation and a lack of attention to utterances that were not relevant to the phenomenon under investigation. The benefits of pilot interviews are critical to study robustness and should involve adherence to the iterative transcribing and analysis practices associated with the phenomenographic approach. When possible, it is helpful to seek feedback from experienced researchers.

For most qualitative approaches, criteria such as 'credibility', 'transferability', 'dependability' and 'confirmability' (Lincoln and Guba 1985: 301–328) is still a test of 'trustworthiness' of the data presented. These had been established by qualitative researchers in response to criticism of quantitative scientists about the merits of their work. We mention them here because you might come across them in the phenomenographic literature, especially if you read some of the earlier studies. Spencer et al proposed four guiding quality principles for evaluating qualitative research, stating that it should be:

> contributory in advancing wider knowledge or understanding; defensible in design by providing a research strategy which can address the evaluation questions posed; rigorous in conduct through the systematic and transparent collection, analysis and interpretation of qualitative data; and credible in claim through offering well-founded and plausible arguments about the significance of the data generated.
> (Spencer et al 2003: 6)

In a more recent article, Tracy (2010: 840) proposed eight criteria as seals of quality: worthy topic; rich rigour; sincerity; credibility;

resonance; significant contribution; ethical considerations; and meaningful coherence. A recent phenomenographic PhD project by Baughan (2019) tried to integrate Tracy's (2010) criteria with the longer established reliability and validity standards. In a book about the doctoral system, Bowden and Green (2019: 105–107) offered these universal hallmarks of research integrity: 'honesty; integrity, responsibility and accountability; good stewardship; and fairness, care and respect for others'.

Phenomenography, while respecting of other qualitative research traditions, has developed its own framework of standards. Åkerlind (2005d: 330–331) described how 'validity' in phenomenography can take the form of two different considerations, namely communicative and pragmatic validity. In terms of reliability, phenomenographers operationalise both coder and dialogic reliability checks, each of which are addressed in the following sections.

Validity

Aspects of validity observed in phenomenography can be broken down into two distinct variations – communicative validity and pragmatic validity – and need to be observed throughout the lifetime of a project. Communicative validity involves open and transparent discourse, usually in the form of an academic conversation, where conflicting knowledge claims can be tested, debated and argued (Brinkmann and Kvale 2015: 288). As a novice researcher, presenting a paper to the phenomenographic community at a conference or publishing in peer-reviewed journals are valuable sources of sense-checking and feedback. Åkerlind (2005d: 330) cautioned against seeking responses from the community of research participants since at the heart of phenomenographic research is the interpretation of the different ways of understanding participants' utterances as a group or as a whole rather than utterances for one individual. Sandberg (2000: 14) demonstrated how they achieved communicative validity by using only two principal open-ended questions, so that interviewees could decide for themselves what in their view was central to the phenomenon as they understood it. When it came to analysing and interpreting individual statements, Sandberg looked at how they corresponded with surrounding comments, and the wider transcript itself.

Pragmatic validity dictates that knowledge is action and that our knowledge claims should be judged by the effectiveness of action (Brinkmann and Kvale 2015: 291). In practical terms this could take the form of follow-up questions that prompt interviewees to relate their statements to what happens in real-life scenarios. Furthermore, comparing these statements with what can be gleaned when the researcher observes participants, in, for example, real-world environments (Sandberg 2000: 14). The emphasis here is on how useful and meaningful the results are to the audience, and goes further than communicative validity, in that there is a stated 'commitment to act' on the findings (Brinkmann and Kvale 2015: 292). Three overall criteria for the validity of the quality of the outcome space are provided in the early literatures, where Marton and Booth (1997: 125) pointed out how pivotal it is that each category conveys a distinctive way of understanding a phenomenon; that the categories are logically related (often, but not necessarily, in a hierarchical manner); and that the critical variation in the data was depicted in as few categories as feasible.

Reliability

As outlined earlier in this chapter, the epistemological perspective of phenomenography is one of intentionality, which means that the researcher must also disclose how they have dealt with their own intentional relation to the individuals' conceptions being investigated (Sandberg 1997). According to Sandberg (1997), reliability as interpretive awareness derived from phenomenological reduction, addressed by recognising and stating the researcher's interpretations at every stage of the research project. For a novice researcher, this 'standing back' can initially be experienced as difficult (see Hornung's account in Chapter 4). During data collection, it is imperative to ask 'what' and 'how' questions, with gentle probing and follow-up questions where relevant, in a manner that affords the interviewee with opportunities to delve deeper into their statements. Central to this is a holding back or the ability to contain one's perceptions and understandings of the phenomenon under investigation (Sandberg 2000). Furthermore, treating all statements as equally important in the early stages of analysis is significant to interpretive rigour. While it can be challenging, Åkerlind (2012: 125) outlined how 'coder reliability check', where researchers independent of each other code interviews and compare their findings, and 'dialogic reliability', which involves critiquing each other's data and interpretations, was practiced often in phenomenographic studies. Durden (2016: 15) used both in their PhD work, putting aside a sample of written responses which they looked at later, comparing them to the emerging categories. They also, after three cycles of analysis, drafted in a second researcher, who independently appraised the data, resulting in a high degree of inter-judge reliability (88 per cent of answers were put into the same category).

Some studies also mention 'replicability' and 'transferability'. Regarding replicability, Marton addressed this question early on in his work, distinguishing between the original act of discovery of conceptions or categories and the later stage, when other scholars should be able to find and recognise the same conceptions or categories once they had been identified by the original researcher (intersubjective agreement) (Marton 1986: 35). Inter-judge reliability has been discounted by Sandberg (1997: 211), however, who argued it was grounded in objectivism and did not respect the researcher's methods and thoughts, hence his proposition of reliability as interpretive awareness.

Transferability

As Kumar (2019: 276) explained, transferability related to the extent to which results gained in one qualitative study can be transferred to different settings or contexts. This is somewhat more complex when engaged in phenomenography, where context is an essential ingredient. One way of addressing this, according to Collier-Reed et al, is to

> analyse the essential aspects of the origin, context, and structure of a research situation so that it is possible for similarities and differences to be seen in relation to other situations where the results are potentially of relevance. For example, this may include providing

analytical tools with which another context can be analysed to be more thoroughly compared with the original setting. In so doing, the framework for the transferability of results is explicitly articulated. (Collier-Reed et al 2009: 12)

Marshall and Rossman (2006: 202) suggest that transferability can be obtained by tying data collection and analysis into the original theoretical framework. Our overarching view aligns with the view of Kettunen and Tynjälä (2018: 7), that 'in phenomenographic studies, it is essential to reflect on the findings' transferability by examining the situational and contextual features that might have coloured the research participants' experiences. The researcher's responsibility is to provide sufficient details to enable the reader to judge the study's transferability'.

Pause and reflect exercise

1. What topic in your field interests you and would benefit from investigating?

2. Narrow this down to research question(s), using 'why' or 'how' type questions.

3. Outline a rough design framework, including all aspects of the approach, and a rationale for each decision made.

4. Articulate your ethics and procedures, and what are or might be the implications for people participating in your project.

5. How will you mitigate risks to your participants and their contributions/data?

6. List the ways in which you will address positionality, trustworthiness, validity and reliability.

7. What might be your next steps?

4

Data generation in phenomenographic work

Similar to other qualitative research approaches, data generation is the practice through which the researcher can and does enter into the subjective life of research participants; those who have experienced or have experiences of phenomena that correspond with and respond to the research question or questions. While research data practices are largely described as 'data collection' across research literatures, we offer what we believe to be an important distinction. Data collection relates more to documentary data, or data that already exists in an information format. Data generation reflects a more participatory exchange of ideas and experiences that are surfaced, transcribed and collated into raw data form. Sandelowski and Barroso situated this divergence as a 'philosophical difference', proposing that:

> data collection implies an independent existence for data, while data generation implies that data have no independent existence apart from the researchers who decide that some things and not others will become data for their projects, and from the specific encounters between researchers and the people and events that are the subjects and objects of study that produce those data. (Sandelowski and Barroso 2002: 214)

Wolcott (1994 cited in Sandelowski and Barroso 2002: 214) strongly agreed, explaining that within the 'data transformation' space 'everything has the potential to be data ... but nothing becomes data without the intervention of a researcher'. While accepting that both terms are used interchangeably within the broader qualitative literature, observing data generation as an exchange and participatory type activity seemed to align more comfortably with our view of ethical research practices.

Data generation, the focus of this chapter, will again be located within the philosophical underpinnings of the phenomenographic stance, that 'there are not two worlds: a real, object world, on the one hand, and a subjective world of mental representations, on the other. There is only one world, a really existing world, which is experienced and understood in different ways by human beings. It is simultaneously objective and subjective' (Marton 2000: 102–116), and indeed, how, as phenomenographers, we get to that, in and through our research work. As is the case in previous chapters, we will present examples and illustrations, where relevant, from our doctoral work and from the work of other qualitative researchers and phenomenographers. We continue to use a mix of textual, verbatim and visual information as a means to providing concrete examples for you, the reader, to work with, as you too journey through the philosophy and practices of phenomenography.

The data generation method associated with and favoured in phenomenographic work so far primarily takes the form of a semi-structured interview, constructed to elicit conceptions of experiences about the phenomena of interest, or how it is conceived of by research participants. The nature of the semi-structured interview in phenomenographic work will thus be given due attention, because of the dimensions and nuances involved in and surrounding the method. In particular, how the researcher is responsible for managing and retaining the

> focus on the way in which interviewees understand the chosen concept and that this focus is maintained throughout the interview. Interviewees are encouraged to express their qualitative understanding of the phenomena under investigation. The researcher may ask interviewees to clarify what they have said and ask them to explain their meaning further. (Bowden 2000: 9–10)

Also, because 'what is needed is a reflexive approach that takes into account the social relationship between researchers and their informants and the constructed nature of the research interview' that is, and will have, psycho-social and dynamic aspects (Richardson 1999: 70). As explained, however, by Thomas (2009: 158), an issue for consideration is that any research method is 'a way of doing something' ... not 'rigidly or formally' ... but something that is 'done in a considered, thought-through way'.

Furthermore, and important to note, is how semi-structured interviews in phenomenographic work can and often do follow on from what is known as a trigger, 'spark', task, event or activity (Turner and Noble 2015: 1). This is a method used to locate, or bring into focus, the phenomenon of interest for study participants. It is designed to be meaningful and immersive, and to lead effortlessly into the semi-structured interview that follows. Reed (2006: 5) described how 'a typical phenomenographic study would first have people perform a task or engage in some activity. ... Thereafter they [participants] would report on it and describe how they had gone about this task or activity'. This was the case, as mentioned previously, in the earliest phenomenographic study on record by Marton, where students were invited to engage in a reading activity related to the subject of their studies. The researchers, in an attempt to reveal variation in approaches to learning, then asked the same group of students about how they had gone about the reading task (Marton 1975).

The focusing activity and semi-structured interview method will be addressed within the sections that directly follow, offering as wide a view as is possible on interviewers, interviews and interviewees, within the space available. This begins with the trigger activity or spark event, which precedes the semi-structured interview when employed as part of the phenomenographic data generation approach. Both are important and relevant to understand, because as Tight (2016: 320) pointed out, 'phenomenographers adopt a particular (albeit with some variations) methodological strategy for data collection and analysis. This typically involves the use of interviews as a method for collecting data on the phenomenon of current interest; though other forms of data, such as written responses, may also be used'.

Trigger, spark, task, event or activity

As noted, this involves the crafting of a focusing activity designed to precede and work towards the semi-structured interview. This operates as a mechanism of focus and provides important anchor and reference points for both the participant and the interviewer, as they move on, into and through the semi-structured interview space. Marton and Booth (1997: 130) urged phenomenographers to notice, and act upon, any ambiguity that might exist for participants, so that 'the phenomenon that the [person] is being asked to handle is ... brought to awareness by the interviewer in an open and concrete form'. In doing so, Turner and Noble (2015: 1) chose to use an arts-type activity 'to describe the conceptions of the experience of early childhood educators with the impact of regulation on their pedagogy and practices'. Their work was informed by Walsh (2000: 19), who mentioned how including 'some predetermined leading experiences and leading prompts ... to focus the interview appropriately for the aims of the study in question' could be of benefit. Furthermore, they reflected on the influence of Weber, who provided 'five suggestions around how images can be utilised as components of inquiries':

- production of images as data,
- using existing images as a springboard,
- to provoke other data,
- to be used as feedback,
- modes of interpretation. (Weber 2008 cited in Turner and Noble 2015: 5)

Turner and Noble (2015: 1) neatly explained the approach they took to the focusing activity as 'methodological elaboration'.

A further example (Figures 4.1 and 4.2) of the use of a focusing activity was developed in anticipation of participants experiencing the phenomena of interest as 'troublesome' or 'knowledge that is

Figure 4.1: Focusing activity

Source: Taylor-Beswick (2019: Appendix 6)

conceptually difficult, even "alien"' (Perkins 1999 cited in Kiley and Wisker 2009: 432). The focusing activity in this research took the form of a mapping tool, adapted with permissions from the work of White and Le Cornu (2011). This was developed to settle the social work student participants into the research environment and to familiarise them with the phenomena of interest.

In this research, the tool was circulated in advance of the scheduled interviews, as a part of the study information pack, which included details about the origins of the tool and user instructions as well as the phenomena of interest (Taylor-Beswick 2019: Appendix 3 and 6). Providing participants with this information meant that once within the interview space the tool and task could seem much less alien and more familiar.

Time was built in to revisit the tool, and the task, and to complete the mapping (Figure 4.2), and in keeping with the phenomenographic approach 'the phenomenon of interest … [was] explored, jointly between the interviewer and interviewee'

Figure 4.2: Completed focusing activity

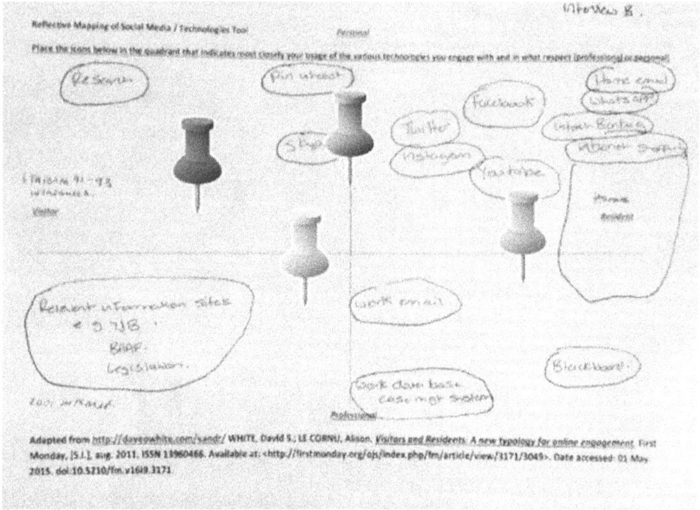

Source: Taylor-Beswick (2019)

(Sin 2010: 312). The process of reflecting on digital tools, choices and behaviours provided access to more specific and detailed accounts of experiences of the digital, throughout the students' professional learning journeys. The conceptions that were presented appeared to have been previously unsurfaced, described, for the first time, by this group of students in terms such as:

> 'When I came on this course no one told us much, if anything at all, about technologies. There was no formal training.'
> 'There are far too many assumptions made about what we know [with reference to digital technologies] and what we can do with all this stuff.'
> 'No, none at all [referring to formal teaching and instruction] and that meant you didn't really know how to use them [technologies] properly.' (Taylor-Beswick 2019: 82)

This example demonstrates the value there is in considering the use or need for a focusing activity as part of the interview design process. The activity needs to centre the phenomena of interest, so that conceptions of experience can start to be surfaced, and so that participants can feel more ready to move into the semi-structured interview.

Significant, and central, to this study was 'gaining a perspective on experiences of digital development, from social work students as recipients of social work education, a process that involved "listening to and learning directly from them" (Hessenauer and Zastrow 2013), through the creation of a space where they could share their experiences and their points of view' (Taylor-Beswick 2019: 2). Marton and Booth (1997: 111) explained that 'in order to make sense of how people handle problems, situations, the world, we have to understand the way in which they experience the problems, the situations, the world that they are handling'. We also need to bear in mind, as Holstein and Gubrium (1995: 14) pointed out, how the 'interview and its participants are constantly developing'. What is also worth noting, in the context of student and education orientated studies, and through a values lens, is that, as Blair made clear,

> feedback from students is not an exact science – it is drawn from the specific experiences of individual students. Such data can be messy to gather and difficult to interpret but that does not mean it should not be valued. The 'easy' response to feedback from students is to find the errors in it. The difficult response to feedback from students is to realise that what they are giving voice to is of genuine concern to them and that this matters. (Blair 2017: np)

We believe this position resonates strongly with the intentions of phenomenographic research work, given how it is designed and facilitated to surface a study participant's point of view, and thereafter report on 'the collective experiences' of a phenomenon of interest (Leadbetter and Bell 2018: 469). Also, as Åkerlind's (2008: 633) work, which sought to understand the nature of teaching and learning, emphasised, seeking 'a teacher-centred understanding' has the potential to undermine understanding what might be 'happening for the students', which is more often than not 'taken-for-granted and not explicitly attended to'. This, of course, could also be the case in other circumstances, where traditionally marginalised groups, such as those with protected characteristics, or those experiencing exclusion or poverty, have little input into research projects, with their views therefore sidelined.

Phenomenographic interviewers, interviews, interviewees

For us, the key characteristics of a good or effective qualitative interviewer are bound up in the abilities necessary to engage and establish rapport with research participants, where 'the key criteria for judging an interview are whether or not it gives access to the participant's lifeworld' (Ashworth and Lucas 2000: 304). There have been legitimate concerns, however, about the process of building rapport and the question of informed consent itself. Duncombe and Jessop (2012: 112) demurred how interviewees might be swayed to reveal personal information because of their perceived 'faked' friendship with the researcher. Consequently, they might not dare question the interview itself, which would weaken the authenticity of informed consent. Rapport building can even start before the interview itself and continue well into the wrap-up phase, with digital technologies making connections easier and more immediate (Miller 2017: 85). Researchers can counteract any of these influences on data collection by documenting and reflecting on research practices including interactions with interviewees (Miller 2017: 86). During her PhD work, Hornung (2010) kept reflective field journals, where she recorded her thoughts and feelings after each interview, constantly learning about her approach to interviewing. She also referred back to them during the transcription process (see Chapter 5).

The capacity for empathy and active listening are deeply significant, where focus and awareness are central to how successfully the interviewer hosts the combined research/ personal life-space. Sjöström and Dahlgren (2002: 341) drew to attention how phenomenographic interviews shared some of the particularities of the 'psychoanalytical interview', in that the interviewer takes an honest, active and non-judgmental interest in what the participant is saying. This approach requires the cognitive capacity to facilitate participants to think aloud and express their views thoroughly, and also provide them with the time to pause and to reflect on the issue of focus. Reflecting on the goal of qualitative interviewing, Seidman (2013: 27) stressed that 'if the interview structure works to allow them [the participants] to make sense to themselves as well as the interviewer, then it has gone a long way toward validity'. To us, this can be implicit within the work, but not often made explicit when reporting on phenomenographic research methods, particularly at the time of data generation.

Developing the interview outline

The following verbatim example (Box 4.1) demonstrates how, through proactive and pragmatic reflexivity, the research aims and interview questions can be reworked, redeveloped and/or refined. As is often the case, and as Marton (1988: 154) pointed out, 'different interviews may follow somewhat different courses'. The explicitness of reporting in this research also works to illustrate how what one sets out to do might bear little resemblance to the final product. There are various reasons for this, such as that acquiring knowledge through using the method leads to a marked increase in one's phenomenographic abilities.

Box 4.1: Developing research and interview questions

The aims of the study changed slightly over time. The initial objectives as stated in the research proposal were as follows:

- to determine the current rate of participation of one-person library (OPL) librarians in CPD
- to establish all current offers of continuing professional development (CPD) for OPL librarians in Ireland
- to show their interest for a different kind of CPD culture they presumably have
- to investigate alternative ways of CPD for OPLs in Ireland

They served as a guide to the researcher during the preliminary literature review by setting loose boundaries on what material could be investigated in more detail. She also explored them with other Library and Information

Studies (LIS) researchers and professionals at her first poster presentation at an international conference. The researcher identified a lack of research investigating the opinions and personal experiences of participants. She therefore revisited her preliminary objectives in the light of her deepening understanding of the field. Many of the other projects had essentially an implied understanding of what CPD was without questioning whether the participants shared that view. This, however, was counterproductive in the researcher's view as it could restrict respondents' answers to already well-known categories without allowing their own voices to be heard. The focus of the research therefore became OPLs' own perceptions of what constituted successful CPD for them and their experience of different means of CPD.

This was fine-tuned into two research questions which captured the core of what the study tried to find out:

1. What are the Irish OPL librarians' conceptions of successful and effective CPD?
2. How do OPLs in Ireland experience different methods of CPD?

The researcher assumed that the librarians would have different perceptions of CPD depending on their experiences and circumstances. This meant that there would be some variation of conceptions. The data analysis revealed that conceptions of these OPLs of CPD could be grouped into five different categories of description and that their experience of different methods of CPD depended on these categories. Two outcome spaces, which presented the findings graphically, were formed to answer the research questions.

Furthermore, three other questions had also developed out of the original objectives as outlined above as a result of further reading, some of which became interview questions:

3. What do OPLs in Ireland think about the levels of support they do receive and what is their perception of barriers to CPD?
4. What would they like to see changed in terms of CPD provision through their organisation, their professional associations and LIS schools?
5. Is there a need for a national policy on CPD for librarians?

Question five tackled an issue that the researcher felt very strongly about and was informed by her continued reading of policies in other countries.

She felt that a national policy on CPD for librarians in Ireland could be the appropriate way forward. The need for an Irish policy was predicted to be an outcome of this research project. Although not explicitly discussed as an interview question with the OPLs, many librarians brought up this topic themselves during the interview or even during the more informal chat before and after.

Source: Hornung (2010: 7–9)

What can initially be experienced as a problem or an issue in terms of the development or redevelopment of the research aims, interview structure or questions can often result in a different and better phenomenographic project. This was shown in Box 4.1 in Hornung's research where she channelled some of her initial objectives into two manageable research questions that had been shaped by her immersion into the wider literature. Thus being open to the ebb and flow of qualitative research helps to situate iteration as integral to the research process, rather than something of an irritation or a flaw in one's approach or the design process.

Phenomenographic interview schedule

This should primarily involve open-ended and gentle probing type questions (Åkerlind 2022), and it is standard practice to develop and deploy an interview guide or interview schedule (Box 4.2). Interview outlines can serve a number of purposes, such as, as an aide memoire, areas to be explored and questions to be asked, and of course must be clearly related to the phenomenon under study. This interview method is also helpful as a prompt to bring respondents gently back to the phenomenon of interest if or when they veer too far off topic. What must be avoided is what Nelson-Jones (2011: 7), in the field of counselling, helpfully described as 'rigidity', where the interview schedule or guide becomes a script to be followed. The ability to be thrown off course, for example, where the order and or wording of questions need to change, is an issue to manage and is associated with the ability to focus and to manage the flow of the interview environment. The interviewer needs to be alert to these possibilities and have the skills to flex accordingly, and at the same time remain aware of what the interviewee is concentrating on, or what both need to concentrate on together (Go and Pang 2021).

Box 4.2: Interview schedule

1. What is your understanding (perception) of the term 'Continuing Professional Development' or 'CPD'?
2. Please describe a situation in which you felt a lack of knowledge (an information need) and of an example of CPD that helped you to address this perceived need.
3. Who in your opinion is responsible for CPD in a one-person library? Why?
4. What barriers, if any, did you have as an OPL experience with regards to CPD? What kind of incentives?
5. Reflecting on your own experience, how important do you think CPD will be for your own future/for the future of the LIS profession?
6. Coming back to my first question: What is your understanding (perception) of the term? What does the term 'CPD' mean in your view?
7. Is there anything else you think I should have asked you? Is there anything you would like to add?

Source: Hornung (2010: 131)

It is useful to follow Patton's (2002) advice of interrogating the interviewee's understanding of a particular phenomenon first and then following up with questions about the descriptions they have offered. This is also in line with the phenomenographic approach, and how the 'specific design feature of the questions in phenomenographic interviews [is] that they should [...] direct the interviewees towards the phenomenon ...' (Bruce 2004: 146).

Phenomenographic interview questions and questioning

Regarding types of questioning, we would suggest that probing and clarifying are extremely helpful interviewing methods. For example, questions such as 'could you tell me more about ...'

or 'what do you mean by that?' can afford participants with opportunities to pause and to expand should they need to or the researcher wants them to expand. This is an approach that often leads to fuller articulations of real-life examples, which can also help participants to elaborate on and or untangle experiences. The use of 'w' questions, such as 'why', can assist with eliciting intentions behind comments and statements (Åkerlind et al 2005: 80). Entwistle (2018) utilised an interactive, almost psychodynamic, form of interviewing, that involved reflecting back to the participants what they had conveyed about their experiences. This is similar to interactions within the psychoanalytical interview, where paraphrasing is reported to evoke a deeper contemplation of experience, and participants are supported to elaborate on and clarify their thinking, as prompted here by the researcher (Nelson-Jones 2011).

To a novice researcher, there are a few potential stumbling blocks within the interview environment, some of which are easier to avoid or address than others. Responding to what an interviewee is saying, yet keeping an overall focus, can be difficult for the early career researcher. So can refraining from asking questions that are leading or desisting from answering the questions for the participants. Another issue that can arise is when the researcher student is conducting a study in their professional field, where it can be hard to avoid being influenced by previous knowledge and assumptions. Watson (2019) argued that depending on the topic under investigation this influence could have undesirable consequences, citing the example of erroneous conceptions of patient safety. Watson adopted a reflexive approach to acknowledging prior in-depth knowledge of the discipline they were working in, that included highlighting potential influences on the research findings. This is why we, like others, stress the importance of addressing positionality and testing your questioning abilities, through, for example, pilot interviews. Also, and as Sjöström and Dahlgren (2002) warned, the interviewer's role in interpreting what the respondent is disclosing requires more than constant attention. There is a need to understand your capacity for swift decision-making, so that, when necessary, the most appropriate type of follow-up question is chosen. This ensures that the questions allow the participant to reflect on their answers using their own mental frameworks and not that of the researcher (Entwistle 1997: 132).

During times where it is hard to maintain the interview focus, there is a risk that the conversation descends into general 'chit-chat'. This is an issue associated with the interview dynamic that should be prepared for, through tuning into oneself and to each of the participants. The outcome grid of the previously mentioned 'a priori criteria sampling' (Hornung 2010: 139) could offer a further advantage if used as a mechanism to tune into any possible participant, researcher or participant–researcher dynamics. 'Tuning-in' can be used purposely, as it is in psychoanalytic interviews, as a means of forecasting and or countering issues of transference or countertransference (Egan 2017: 103). This has a place in the qualitative research environment (Smith 2008). It is in these circumstances where the use of a field journal can be helpful, as a means to capturing thoughts and feelings, pre, during and post the research interview. Indeed, Sin (2010: 314) described how 'a careful researcher should mitigate losing touch with the original interview contexts by reflecting on the interviews shortly afterward', a time when 'mental and written notes of relevant contextual features of the interviews' can be accurately made.

As previously mentioned, for the writing of this book, we revisited the varied and many tensions we experienced throughout our 'becoming' phenomenographers. As associated with the matter of interviewer and interview dynamics, we discussed the tensions of over-identification and/or over-familiarity, natural aspects when people form together in a relational context or in a relational manner. Again, these are psychoanalytic phenomena that require the interviewer to notice and to have the skills to politely deflect or redirect the conversation (Esterberg 2002), say, for example, where the interviewee seeks to draw the interviewer to offer a view on the experience of focus or on a personal matter. It is in these moments that a quick glance at the interview guide, schedule, the completed trigger, or spark task, can help to refocus and recentre the interviewer and enable them to proceed with purpose. Gorman and Clayton (2005: 195) denoted qualitative research as being 'both an art and a science'. Interviewing requires the interviewer to be able to relate to people and to have the capacity to remain tuned into what they are saying. Seidman's (2013: 30–31) advice was to practice by interviewing fellow researchers and be open to being interviewed by them in return: 'the practice project should alert you to how the way you are as a person affects your interviewing'.

Other methods of data generation are employed, some of which can be found in phenomenographic research representing innovative and creative examples. The following are a small selection of those that have stood out for us when adding to our research knowledge repertoire and which you might find interesting and helpful. In no particular order, beginning with Wihlborg (2005), who deployed the survey method using questions based on data derived from previous interviews with participants. Content analysis was combined with a qualitative analysis approach inspired by phenomenography. Concept maps and semi-structured interviews were utilised by Yu (2019), who asked participants to manually draw a simplified concept map by listing several key concepts that they thought were important to 'being a doctor'. Semi-structured interviews were used to probe these understandings further, to gauge participants' overall conceptions. Edwards (2007) successfully applied 'think alouds' in their study on university students' experiences of web-based information searching while capturing participants' interactions on video. The aim was to identify any triggers that prompted students to move from one level of searching to a higher, more sophisticated level. Edwards began by giving students written questions and then asked them during the interviews to elaborate verbally on the answers they had recorded on paper. These formed a focusing activity. As part of the conversation, the researcher requested the students to recall a recent searching incident to focus their minds on relevant, recent learning activities (Edwards 2007: 94–95). After these interviews, participants searched online for a specific topic and reflected on what they were doing. By using this method, Edwards collected rich data combining written documents with data transcribed from both audio and video tapes. McGuigan (2017: 121) wanted to afford participants the freedom to reflect on their experiences. Therefore, data collection took place in the form of:

- a focus group in which participants created a collage;
- through semi-structured interviews;
- the use of reflective diary activities;
- creating photographic objects posted to a Facebook site.

Lister (2022: 72) adapted the interview techniques from their learning of conducting semi-structured interviews. They introduced phenomenographic style group discussions into their classroom with only minimal probing from the researcher. This novel learning approach allowed students to reflect on what they had learned, why, how, and even where it might have happened. Qualitative phenomenographic results could be further analysed using quantitative statistical methods. Recently, Feldon and Tofel-Grehl (2022) made the case for fully integrated mixed methodology. They outlined previous studies which had developed survey instruments and suggested adding latent class analysis and item response theory into the mix.

As can be seen, the range of methods deployed to surface experiences of phenomena in various populations and contexts are diverse, creative and reassuringly true to phenomenographic methodology. There are many more studies and authors that we would have referred to in much more detail, if we had more space, and we refer to our 'further reading' section at the end of this book. We would just like to mention Straub (2020: 49), who felt 'it was important that I consider the multiple realities experienced by the participants. To do this, I used multiple sources of qualitative data, including interviews, observations, and documents'. We would highly recommend reading at least some of the work outlined, given how and what it adds to the fabric of phenomenographic learning and literatures, and so can help the emerging phenomenographer. In addition, if one is completely new to this type of data generation practice, we list resources at the end.

In closing, one of the most important things to remember when designing, engaging and steering the data generation process is that the interview is open and deep:

> the interview is open means that while a structure might be planned in advance, to approach the phenomenon

in question from various interesting perspectives, the interviewer is prepared to follow unexpected lines of reasoning that can lead to fruitful new reflections. That the interview is deep means that particular lines of discussion are followed until they are exhausted, and the two parties have come to a state of mutual understanding. (Booth 1997: 138)

We cannot stress enough how important it is to remain close to the principles and practices of key and established phenomenographic thinkers and practitioners, especially in the early years of becoming a phenomenographer. It is this we recall as having had the most impact on our confidence, and on our ability to stretch and flex our own phenomenographic wings.

Pause and reflect exercise

1. What type of data generation method would be appropriate for your research project?
2. Would a trigger or spark event be something that would be needed or useful?
3. How might you draft an interview schedule?
4. What is your knowledge of interview questions and questioning?
5. How will you manage the dynamics and focus within the interview space?

5

Phenomenographic transcription and data analysis

There are a number of standard and very well-established transcription and data analysis practices in qualitative research, that in general terms involve the transcribing of interviews and the application of an analytical method or framework aligned to the research question(s) and the insights sought. While there is thought to be no 'best way' or 'right answer' when designing and undertaking research practices, there are some helpful methods of working with transcripts and navigating data analysis within the phenomenographic context. It is these unique practices that will be the focus this chapter, that, similar to the preceding chapters, includes a mix of information formats, offered to illustrate the approaches we and other phenomenographers have used when engaged with these particular aspects of phenomenographic work.

Before moving on, it is worth noting that while the use of technology has been part of research practices for a significant period, new and emerging technologies are presenting both opportunities and challenges that need to be worked on and worked through. The time-saving efficiencies and data categorisation affordances of newer technologies can lead to problems, particularly in comparison to the more analogue and rudimentary type technologies such as voice recorders or dictaphones. In data protection and data storage terms, analogue technologies are a lot easier to work with and through. The use of transcribing and thematising technologies, without due diligence, can pose a risk to participant privacy and protection assurances. This applies particularly where technology choices and usage involve 'free and low-cost' platforms (McMullin 2023: 140), require working across data laws and 'jurisdictions' (de Villiers et al 2022: 11), or where they are described as 'good enough' data transcription and translation outputs within academic literatures (Bokhove and Downey 2018: 1).

This is why we emphasise the need to apply an ethical lens when considering emerging technological solutions in and for your research practice, given that a significant number of these technologies have not been built for research purposes. This means there is a pressing need for researchers to understand and

> be vigilant about the potential harms ... such as data mining, profiling, and scraping. Such foci for the scholarship of research ethics, and what (in)forms the support, development, and assessment of its quality in practice, is of direct public interest, as is the continued contentious terrain of data protection and privacy. (Belluigi and Taylor-Beswick 2022: 39)

Associated with this is the suggestion by Goldkind et al (2020: 90) that 'the time for transparency has never been more urgent'. Researchers need to understand and be able to articulate to participants, in clear and digestible terms, the implications of engaging with platforms that are not research-specific and are built for commercial usage. Also important are the views of Ellis (2007: 29), who reminded us that ethical practices require 'researchers to act from our hearts and minds, acknowledge our interpersonal bonds to others, and take responsibility for actions and their consequences'. This is significant because technology, technology choices and technology usage are not neutral and therefore need to be given due consideration at every stage of the research process. One final observation is the relatively low-tech nature of our respective projects, and perhaps surprisingly how the mostly highly recommended research software was abandoned in a digitally oriented study (Box 5.1). This was not done for the reasons cited in the preceding paragraph, but due to the researcher's experience of the technology, that was felt to be creating an additional layer between the researcher and data (see Box 5.1). This is, however, not reflective of the wider research community, those who use and those who will go on to use qualitative data analysis software. The benefits, including how these programmes support analytical work, are clearly outlined in literature (see, for example, Kara 2022: 127).

Box 5.1: Transcription and analysis rationale

Given the digital focus of this work, it is significant to include reference to the decision to abandon the use of the digital platform NVivo, post transcribing the interview recordings. Even though this data-analysis software is popular across the research populace (Hoover and Koerber 2009), the decision made was influenced by experiencing the platform as a restrictive context in which to listen, to collate and to make sense of the collective experiences of the student participants. Listening to the audio recordings and annotating the physical transcripts, in hardcopy format, felt more conducive to 'being with' the data. Furthermore, this more manual or physical form of analysis proved helpful to reducing the possibility of, as cautioned by Ashworth and Lucas (2000: 298), moving 'too quickly' through the highly iterative process associated with phenomenographic analysis, in which, as cited above the 'pools of meanings' emerge (Marton 1986: 43). Whilst not in complete agreement with the thoughts of Roberts and Wilson (2002) who explain that 'it is the creative and interpretive stages of qualitative data analysis, requiring human reflection and understanding… that are most difficult to reconcile with the application of ICT (np)', this experience highlights how researchers should not feel pressure to succumb to technological advances, that analytical choices should be made to ensure, as much as is ever possible, that the voices of research participants can be heard (Doucet and Mauthner 2008).

Source: Taylor-Beswick (2019: 78)

This example could be sentimentalised within the current tech-optimism context, as an occurrence in need of 'post-digital' analysis (Fawns et al 2023: np), or a reminder of the value of human-centred physicalness or materiality. There is a significant amount more to say on and about this matter, but in taking Kara's (2020: 171) view about the finiteness of reporting slightly out of context, it is impossible in this work 'to tell everything that needs to be told'. This point is applicable to both research work and the rapidly changing socio-technical world that is consuming all aspects of life and work (Williamson 2021), and rupturing 'existing theories and their continuation' including long-standing and traditional research contraventions and work (Jandrić et al 2018: 895).

Working with the transcripts

When considering data and data analysis, the first decision that needs to be made is the approach to translating the interview material into a workable data format. This includes whether to outsource to an independent transcription service, or an artificial intelligence or some other automated platform, or to do the transcription oneself. There are advantages and disadvantages associated with each of these methods, some of which are discussed widely across research literature (see, for example, Moylan et al 2015; Belluigi and Taylor-Beswick 2022; Rodríguez Bolívar and Alcaide Muñoz 2022; Thunberg and Arnell 2022); with factors such as time constraints, financial considerations, and debates about accuracy and bias. Up until now, and in the current context of the Fifth, or Internet of Things, Revolution, the era of hyperconnectivity, manual or low-tech transcribing by the researcher has generally been strongly recommended. One particular advantage of this method is the immersiveness that manual or low-tech transcribing has conventionally been thought to offer. In phenomenographic terms, and for us, this offers the opportunity to pay closer attention to what was signed, signalled or said, and to revisit what one thought they heard, saw or said. Given also how phenomenography involves multidimensional researcher relationality (Figure 5.1), the significance of this choice supports access into and progress through the various steps involved in the highly iterative data analysis process.

However, and as noted earlier, there is no right or one way of turning interview material into a workable data format, and again there is little discussion about the approach to transcription within phenomenographic literatures. There is, however, a clear sense of how the relational and multisensory physicality associated with

Figure 5.1: Phenomenographic relationality

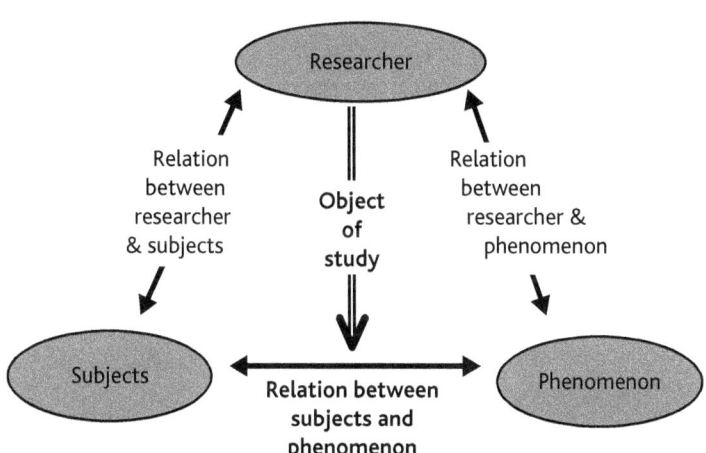

Source: Bowden (2005a: 13)

the act of transcribing can present the researcher with a particular kind of opportunity. What arose for each of us, during and after the transcription process, was realising and an appreciating of how researchers can get closer to participants' conceptions. Transcription takes a phenomenal amount of time, but the value we each experienced cannot be overemphasised, including the benefits of listening and re-listening to the interviews. As reflected, there are benefits 'from a primary familiarisation gained from transcribing the interview recordings, familiarisation that involved re-listening to the interview recordings and the reading and re-reading of the interview transcripts' (Taylor-Beswick 2019: 75).

Whichever method is chosen, in phenomenographic work it is important that the emphasis remains on accuracy, of capturing what has been conveyed by participants, and in a manner that remains true to their voices. Reflexivity as a research practice has more advantages when it is 'maintained throughout the transcribing of the interviews and data analysis; doubling up as both an analytical tool and as a "bracketing" strategy (Mohd-Ali et al., 2016, p.190); a medium for staying as close and true to the student's descriptions of their experiences as possible' (Bowden 2000 in Taylor-Beswick 2019: 76).

We must however acknowledge that the time, if it is not already upon us, may come for fully automated transcription as a generic research practice. Until that time, and within the phenomenographic context, we remain convinced of the value of getting close to the data, and doing so in a manner that is most ethical and effective for you and for your participants. Another point, leading into thinking about data analysis, is that while all forms of transcription afford opportunities to start to consider conceptions, we must avoid drawing conclusions and draft conceptions or categories of description too soon (Bruce 1998). We can and should, however, tune into the 'familiarisation' aspect of transcription cited as part of Dahlgren and Fallsberg's model (1991: 152) and maximise this opportunity to listen to what your participants said and how they said it (as outlined further into the chapter). It is also worth returning to field notes at this point, as one enters into the analytical phase.

Phenomenographic data analysis

The emphasis here will be on semi-structured interviews as they are the most widely used method of data generation. The advantage of in-depth interviews is that they deliver two complementary types of results: evidence of the phenomenon and its contexts, as well as the cultural frames people use for sensemaking (Miller and Glassner 2011: 137). While various methods of working with the transcripts are illustrated throughout phenomenographic literature, there are some more frequently used and cited approaches to analysis that tend to be repeated. For example, the following outline offered by Bruce, who described the overall aim of phenomenographic analysis as:

- becoming familiar with the transcripts;
- determining the qualitatively differing meanings associated with the varying experiences of ... [the phenomenon];
- determining how people's awareness of ... [the phenomenon] was being structured for the meaning to be experienced;
- creating the categories of description; and identifying the relationships between the categories to develop an outcome space. (Bruce 1998: 28)

As stressed by Marton (1986: 42) there have not been exact techniques to aid the researcher, only general descriptions of how other authors have proceeded. Little has changed in this respect, and it is therefore perhaps unsurprising that data handling presents so differently across the literature. There is a considerable amount of variation in practice, as we will illustrate, and unfortunately, particularly for the novice researcher, the detail of the analysis stage is often underreported. Where mentioned, analysis is discussed only briefly, hence our efforts to present a range of different frameworks and processes.

Summarising historic developments, Forster (2016) identified two schools of phenomenographic analysis, labelling them as the 'Marton school' and 'Åkerlind school', respectively, and emphasising that the main difference rested on the role of transcripts. Åkerlind (see, for example, Åkerlind [2005c] for a personal account of analysis) agreed with Bowden on focusing on the whole transcript and to not separate any utterance from its context (Bowden 2005a). She stressed how decontextualising quotes runs the danger of losing the perceived meaning: 'One thing we often found we needed to do was to go back a few pages earlier than the designated page in the transcript and, as well, read forward a few extra pages, if we were to really capture the meaning' (Bowden 2005a: 25). Åkerlind (2005d: 327) argued that the whole manuscript 'should be seen and treated as a set of interrelated meanings, which can best be understood in relation to each other'. In her work, she designed an iterative process:

- Within *individual transcripts*, particular statements were interpreted within the context of the whole manuscript
- Within *groups of similar transcripts* (tentatively representing a category of description), individual transcripts were interpreted within the context of the whole group of transcripts, plus
- Groups of transcripts (or individual categories of description) were interpreted within the context of the *total set of all transcripts* (or categories of description) as a whole. (Åkerlind 2005b: 120; italics in original)

Marton, on the other hand, did not use the transcript itself as a data unit (Forster 2016). Marton (1986) advocated reading and re-reading, or immersion in the transcripts, so that the similarities of the data, in the form of verbatim quotations, can be grouped and regrouped and collected under broad themes, or 'meaning pools'. This two-stage process was outlined in another paper:

> The first stage focused on identifying and describing the conceptions in terms of their *overall meanings*. This is done by marking and segmenting the transcripts according to the themes addressed. A unit was formed whenever there was sufficient evidence that a particular overall meaning has been expressed. The second stage of analysis focused on identifying the *structural aspect* of each conception expressed. The units, now denoted by the various overall meanings, were studied in detail, to identify within each unit the elements of the phenomenon that were focused upon, and to devise a description of each conception's structural aspect. In doing so, we paid attention to the explicit *variations* that the student brought in as they focused on a particular element, as well as the *variations* that were implied by that element. (Marton and Pong 2005: 337; italics in original)

This lengthy quote captures, in valuable detail, the iterative process associated with phenomenographic analysis.

In addition, and elsewhere, Marton elaborates on how his team set about handling the transcripts:

> Quotes are sorted into piles, borderline cases are examined, and eventually the criterion attributes for each group are made explicit. In this way, the groups of quotes are arranged and rearranged, are narrowed into categories, and finally are defined in terms of core meanings, on the one hand, and borderline cases on the other. Each category is illustrated by quotes from the data. (Marton 1986: 43)

Åkerlind (as explained in Åkerlind 2005b: 171), in contrast, used a subset of 17 transcripts out of 28 interviews conducted in order to manage the large amount of data gained. She read them all three times, marked any unrelated phenomena during the second reading, and wrote additional notes about key themes emerging in each manuscript. These were also read as a set, and notes on the similarities and differences were made. Transcripts were then sorted into piles, followed by extensive grouping and regrouping work, which at a later stage was complemented by another re-reading of the notes. Åkerlind also identified 'dimensions of variation' in meanings that were evident across manuscripts. She additionally grouped these into 'themes of expanding awareness', which 'may be seen as representing structural groupings between different dimensions of variation, highlighting the structural relationship between different dimensions' (Åkerlind 2005b: 122). Bruce (1997) also did not physically cut up the manuscripts but rather extracted quotes and other pieces of conversational text at the final stage when engaged in developing the full description of the categories.

Whether a researcher follows one school or the other is in a sense irrelevant since both produce legitimate results. As Collier-Reed and Ingerman (2013) accentuate, even though eminent phenomenographers followed different paths of data analysis, ultimately, these different ways all pointed to the same underlying philosophy. Han and Ellis (2019: 5) highlighted the similarities in key stages of analysis evident in the models offered by Marton et al (1992), Dahlgren and Fallsberg (1991)/McCosker et al (2004) and Säljö (1997), respectively, to emphasise that point. All three schemes started with a familiarisation stage followed by data reduction and condensation, classification of responses, and labelling, although terminology differed slightly from one framework to the next. It is widely known and accepted among the phenomenography community that phenomenographic data analysis is and can be a daunting prospect, with even Marton (1986), the founder of the approach, acknowledging the magnitude of the task. Phenomenographic researchers put effort into producing detailed verbatim accounts in their transcripts to accurately represent the utterances, which add an additional layer of reliability (Sin 2010: 314).

Interviews usually generate a vast number of rich descriptions and to a novice researcher this can seem overwhelming. Therefore phenomenographers, including those new to this approach, are often seen to take a pragmatic approach to the analytical process. Watson (2016) reported applying a mix-and-match type approach in their research, following the analytical framework of Dahlgren and Fallsberg (1991), with elements of Åkerlind's method found to complement the overall process. For a new phenomenographer, we recommend Dahlgren's and Fallsberg's model (1991: 152):

- familiarisation
- condensation
- comparison
- grouping
- articulating
- labelling
- contrasting

because of how it provides an accessible and logical structure to phenomenographic analysis. Others have used software to manage large amounts of data at the early stage of analysis, to help conceptualise and settle into what can feel like an overwhelming task, or one that is unmanageable (Salaz 2015). Some, for example, have used NVivo as a data management tool to facilitate the labelling of text, tags and sub-tags which could then be applied to quickly retrieve groups of snippets and quotations. Grouping and regrouping of text can therefore be made more manageable, and multiple meanings can be attached to the same extract of the transcripts. Unsurprisingly, software tools are experienced differently by different researchers, as illustrated earlier in this chapter (Box 5.1).

Also mentioned earlier, linked to the very nature of phenomenography, is how researchers, like participants, can, and likely will, experience and engage with phenomena differently. Another variation in the approach to data management and analysis is seen in the work of Huntley (2003: 116), who carried out a 'coarse' interim analysis after a superficial scanning of the data. This approach assisted with obtaining an initial sense of how the phenomenon was experienced by the participants. Conversely, Alsop and Tompsett (2006: 247) began with structured reading to identify key aspects of the phenomenon, then tried to capture significant variation for each of these aspects, and finally separated the experiences into levels and clustered them into an outcome space. However, attention should be paid to the work of Bruce (1998: 28), who advised that there are two main views on 'data analysis amongst phenomenographers. In the first, analysis is seen as a construction process; in the second, it is seen as a discovery process'. In addition, they emphasised the problem with adopting either of these approaches in isolation of the other, which is that those who are committed to 'the former view are in danger of imposing a logical framework on their data; and those with the latter are in danger of bypassing the analytical process' (Bruce 1998: 28).

By way of contributing to the lack of explicitness, noted by phenomenographers in and across the literature, about how *to do* phenomenographic data analysis, we offer a detailed account of an analytical process. The following is drawn from an approach taken in the research of one author (Hornung 2010), with reference to the work of others woven throughout (Taylor-Beswick 2019), where this is helpful and/or relevant.

In-depth example of phenomenographic data analysis

One of the first decisions to be made when engaging in data analysis is about the handling of the data, much of which will be based upon personal preference. In the following example the researcher chose a paper-based approach, which involved working with the interview transcripts in print format. As part of this, they deployed a 'cut and paste technique' which allowed them to deal with the sheer amount of data while keeping the context in focus. For reasons of transparency and consistency, the researcher also incorporated handwritten notes captured in a log book (Figure 5.2) as a mechanism to support reflection and decision making. It is worth pointing out that when coding data in qualitative research one needs to use the concept under investigation as the point of focus or the guiding principle. It is also the case that there will be variance in the length of the unit of text drawn from the transcripts (Babbie 2016: 397). The length of the unit of text is associated with the relevance of what has been said in the context of the phenomenon under investigation and in the development of the meaning pools.

Figure 5.2: Log book page

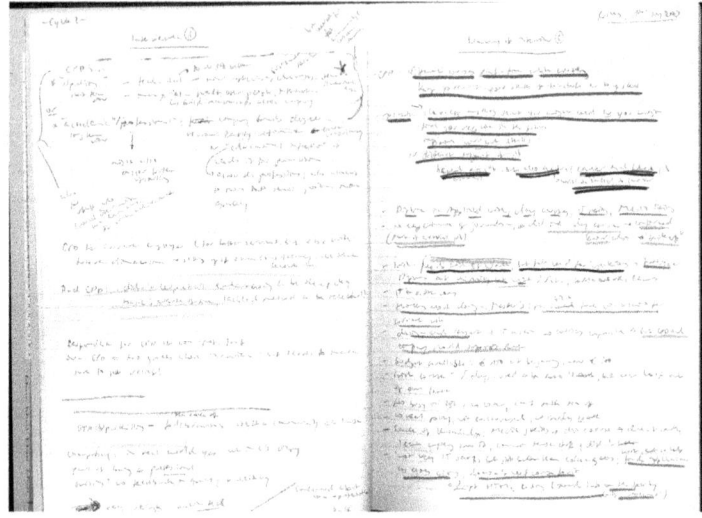

Source: Hornung (2010: np; additional photo)

Two notebooks were filled with summaries and a third with ideas and procedural decisions. In combination, these methods were also found to enrich understandings of what the interviewees had as their focus, and what they concentrated upon. Since the analysis took six months to complete, these detailed memos also functioned as a method of keeping the researcher on track and to chart her progress as a sole researcher. Lapadat (2000: 212) advised including details in the transcripts: the 'tape counter' of the recording to provide a time stamp; 'conversation' to take note of what was said; and 'context' of gestures and mimics to capture non-verbal clues. In Hornung's (2010) study, the researcher changed this last post into 'comments',

> thus keeping track of the circumstances of the interview, which included some gestures, but also interruptions and other occurrences. Body language is an essential part of any type of interaction with other people, so the interviewer took note of gestures, facial expressions, and posture where appropriate, e.g.

about people shifting uncomfortably in their seats or hesitating to answer. Situations like that made her rephrase a question as she did not want participants to have an unpleasant experience. (Hornung 2010: 146)

In research, however, it can be ok for participants to be uncomfortable. What is important is that non-verbal behaviour can suggest there is something worthwhile exploring.

The analysis of qualitative data does not follow an absolute or concrete set of steps. As mentioned previously, it is a cyclical and iterative operation that involves many oscillating and overlapping phases. Hornung (2010: 158) established the following model drawing on some pointers given by Lupton (2008: 73–75).

First cycle of analysis

1. First she wrote summaries of all interviews and tried to capture (in long hand) all statements about continuing professional development (CPD) using the main questions as headings (individual focus).
2. The researcher then looked at the full transcripts, including background questions. Some people revealed more about their experiences after the official interview was over, so she wanted to capture them in the statements (individual focus).
3. She colour-coded (Figure 5.3) a subset of the first five summaries highlighting individual statements (Figure 5.4). Initially, the researcher felt that it would be valuable to continue doing this with the remaining 25 interviews (individual focus) and to put the coded statements into a matrix using Microsoft Word.

It is worth outlining how, at this point, the researcher felt stuck and sought advice from their supervisor, an issue that can be linked to an earlier point we made about how phenomenographic analysis can be experienced as overwhelming. In the present example, the researcher and the advisor agreed on a 'cut and paste' approach as a technique for moving the analysis forward, with photography used for the purposes of capturing and evidencing decisions

Figure 5.3: Index of colour code

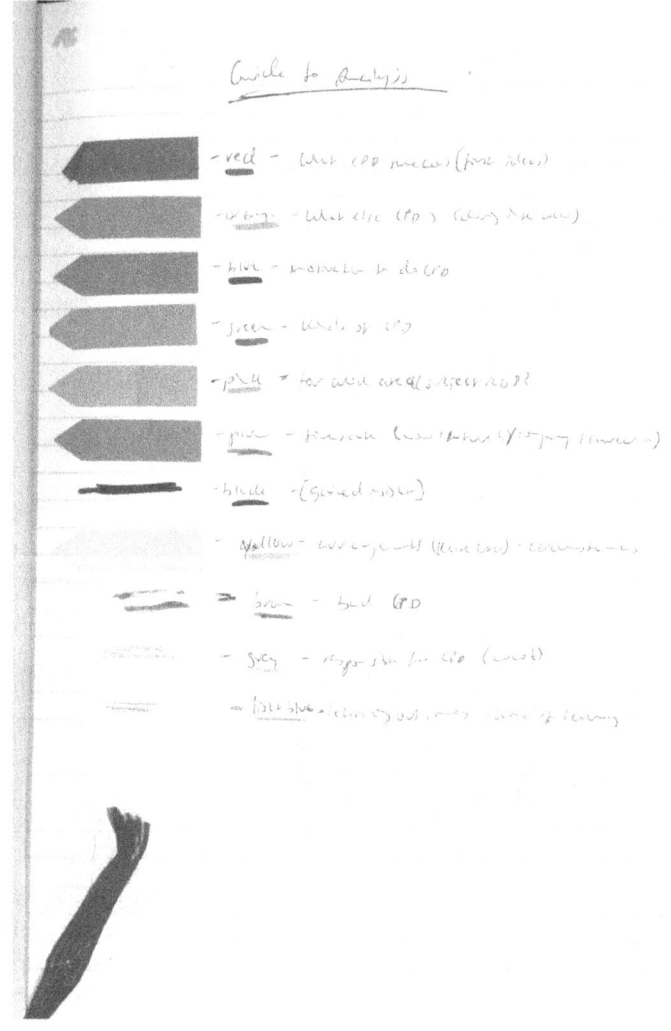

Source: Hornung (2010: 159)

Phenomenographic transcription and data analysis

Figure 5.4: Colour coding statements

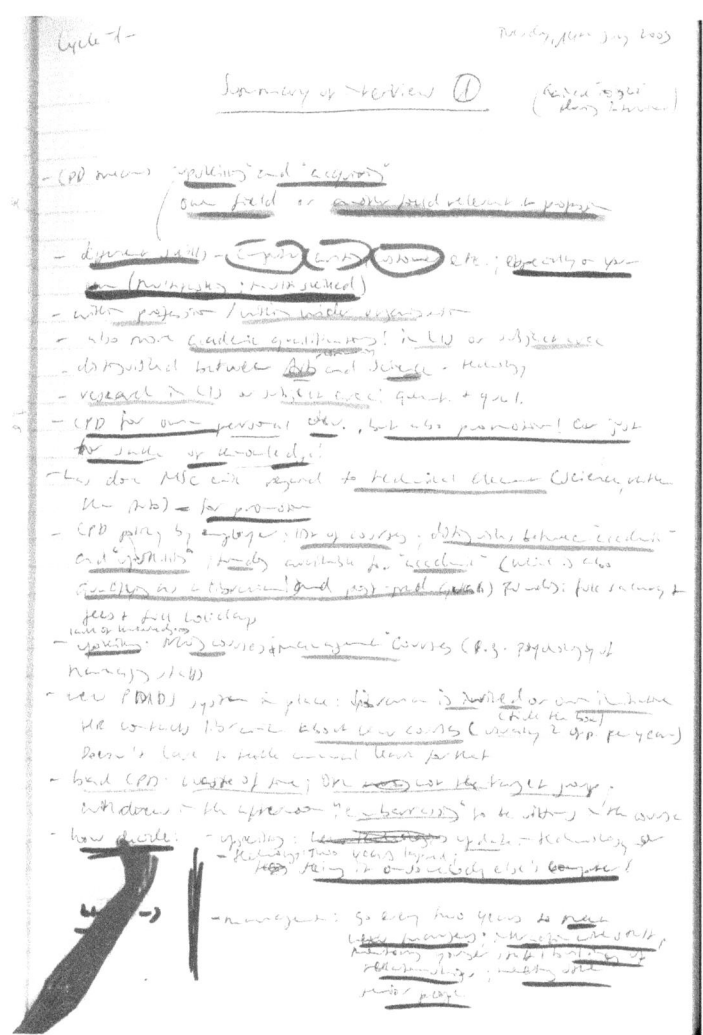

Source: Hornung (2010: 159)

made. Adding this visual evidence, the researcher aimed at being 'as explicit as possible' (Francis 1996: 44), and to show her way of thinking.

Second cycle of analysis

5. The collective experience is at the heart of phenomenography. There will be similarities and differences between people's ways of experiencing the phenomenon of interest, and the intentions behind their words might be different. To manage the vast amount of data (between 20 and 30+ pages per transcript) a subset of five interviews (Figure 5.5) was chosen following Åkerlind's advice (Åkerlind 2005b: 171), which represented different variables, such as gender, location, years of experience and library setting, to keep maximum variation. At a later stage, the remaining 25 interviews were subjected to the same rigorous procedure outlined here.

Figure 5.5: Interview number at each statement

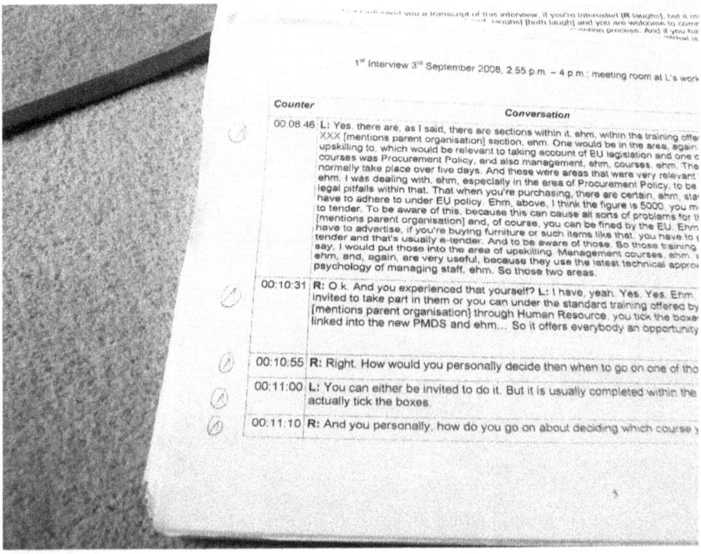

Source: Hornung (2010: 161)

Phenomenographic transcription and data analysis

Figure 5.6: Cutting the interviews along statements

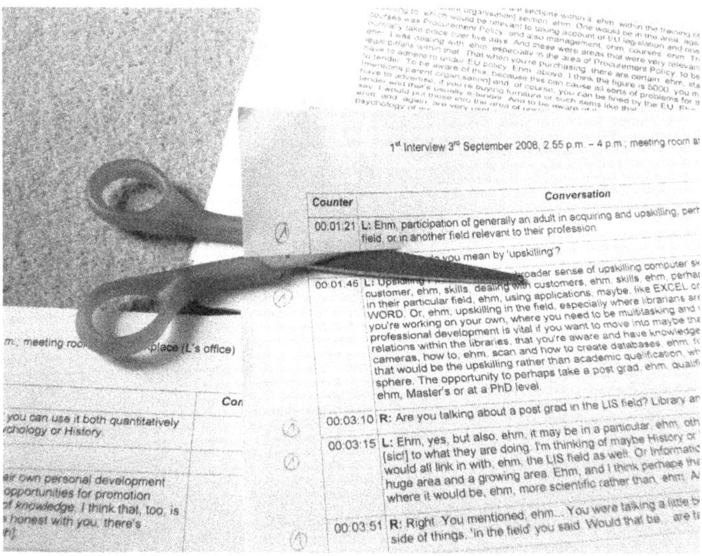

Source: Hornung (2010: 161)

6. The physical handling of the data (the focus here remained at this stage on the individual transcript). The researcher made the decision to cut each of the five physical transcripts along the structure of the questions posed by the interviewer (Figure 5.6), using the research questions as headings under which to group statements. At this point various kinds of groupings quickly started to emerge which formed the base for some initial, albeit very vague categories. These 'categories' became even more apparent as Hornung worked through the remaining 25 and two more categories emerged.

The researcher placed these piles of comments and utterances into plastic folders, highlighting parts of the conversation that made a case for placing it in a particular folder. She gave them initial labels, for example, 'upskilling'. This work was iterative and required a fair amount of reorganisation. The researcher tried to be 'context-sensitive' (Åkerlind 2005d: 331): where a paragraph elaborating on an idea continued onto the next page, it was cut out, stapled

Table 5.1: Emerging categories of description: early stage formulation of category 1

Category	Description	Interview no. (counter)
1	CPD is upskilling – both technical upskilling, which relates to training in management, customer service, technology, and so on (more practical), and academic upskilling, which is my development as librarian, combating 'educational inflation' and possibly promotion and means higher academic qualifications or writing articles. You need both to have a modern, progressive service and to bring the library forward, so that another librarian can take over easily. If librarians are not constantly upskilled, it's a loss to themselves, the staff, and the community at large and you don't have good customer service (service orientation).	1 (13:30), (44:36), (45:36); **14** (01:19), (13:34); **12** (02:22)

Source: Hornung (2010: 351)

to the first sheet and put into the same folder. Where required, the snippets could be traced back to their original contexts.

The emerging categories (group focus)

7. Having re-read each interview again, the researcher tried to construct meaningful statements, for example, 'CPD is successful if …' using the summaries of interviews that had been previously written out in the analysis notebooks. This method was in line with Åkerlind's (2005a) approach. All five interviews were analysed using this method, including re-reading across all of them again (group focus), until the researcher felt that a first set of categories had been established. Following Bowden's (2005b) matrix for developing categories (Table 5.1) helped with keeping track of which conversational snippets seemed to express facets of the same category. Moving through the transcripts the researcher added more examples of utterances and expanded the descriptions.

Revisiting the supervisor at this point provided the researcher with a timely pause to discuss the emerging categories and possible labelling. They read statements to each other to check if the categories were identifiable. Some required more discussion than others, but some were instantly recognisable. After a prolonged debate they agreed on the final categories.

The timing of supervision in this work echoes what Kvale (1996: 248) referred to as 'pragmatic validity' and reflects how qualitative research can be enriched by feedback from other researchers. Åkerlind (2005b) strongly promoted this approach in doctoral work, because of how the sole phenomenographic researcher learns, so acutely, through doing. This was illustrated by Dunkin (2000) in their account of being a lone researcher who worked with a challenger throughout their first study. In contrast, in their second study, they only defended their results towards the end of the analysis process. They felt that this delay in receiving feedback had required higher levels of self-discipline during the analysis process. Clearly, the interaction with other people is key to the researcher's interpretation and understanding of the data, as shown in this practice example, particularly through the probing of the supervisor and another phenomenographic PhD student. Walsh (2000) argued that potential for bias could be managed by a solo researcher specifying their own perceptions and expertise and being open to other researchers checking their initial results. In Hornung's case the relationship with her supervisor helpfully shifted over time from critical friend to 'devil's advocate', which provided the opportunity to provide rationale for and defend the emerging categories. If as a novice researcher one doesn't enjoy that kind of access, it might be useful to discuss early findings with fellow students or as part of a poster presentation at a conference.

Analysis of the remaining interviews

Hornung's analysis of the remaining 25 interviews involved a constant checking for similarities and differences. What was notable about this approach and phase of analysis was the starkness of how some participants' comments fit with other people's comments. Many statements were found to be almost identical and, therefore, throughout this part of the analysis process it was necessary to return to the original transcripts. The writing of meaningful statements took the form of a second, even shorter summary, while working with the manuscripts. The categories changed and expanded in the light of more transcript cut-outs being added and, simultaneously, while developing the table of dimensions (see Chapter 6 for more information).

This example offers one method of working with the data. In other research projects one may come across methods such as Framework Analysis (FA), as was the case in Hornung's (2019) project on librarians with doctorates in libraries. FA was developed by Jane Ritchie and Liz Spencer in the 1980s in order to study applied qualitative research questions within a limited time frame (Pope et al 2000). Other studies have also combined the phenomenographic approach with FA. For example, Visram et al (2014), who investigated conceptions of knowledge translation of public health workers employing focus groups and semi-structured interviews. Venkatasalu et al (2015) examined perceived clinical outcomes of teaching methods. Their participants received classroom and simulation-based teaching and were subsequently interviewed in-depth about their experiences. In the field of library and information studies, Rajapakse and Kiran (2017) explored succession planning in academic libraries through interviews and document analysis. More recently, Wan and Leung (2022) integrated phenomenography with discourse analysis in their study of prospective teachers' conceptions of curriculum leadership. The flexibility of phenomenography extends to both analysis and presentation. Dunkin (2000) included case studies featuring individual voices to supplement their findings based on phenomenographic analysis, which, by their nature, entailed the collective experience of the phenomenon.

To provide a counternarrative for the magnitude of the phenomenographic analytical task or feelings of being overwhelmed, and regardless of the method or combination of methods you choose, it is of value to consider the reflections of Bowden (2005a: 29), who explained: 'something that I have observed every time I have undertaken a phenomenographic analysis remains a source of joy and a motivation to continue with repeated analysis of interview transcripts. The observation is that as you proceed with the analysis, each new reading of the transcript brings new insights'.

The value, richness and importance of the analytical method is not to be underestimated, given what this detailed and iterative analytical method adds to the work, and the reliability and viability that will be sought from those who engage with it. We leave readers with these thoughts because of how they served to develop our confidence, us, and our abilities to work with such a robust analytical method of working with data. We also value those of Kelly (2002: np), who made the important point that we must keep 'conceptualisations faithful to individuals' conceptualisations' of the phenomenon. Analysis of this nature aids phenomenographers to evade 'taken-for-granted' assumptions about what may arise as the focus of awareness for participants (Ashworth and Lucas 2000 cited in Taylor-Beswick 2019: 81). 'Faithfulness' is how (Reed 2006: 3) appropriately framed this, and this is a philosophy that continues on into the structuring and presenting of findings.

Pause and reflect exercise

1. Which analytical school of thought do you lean towards and why?

2. What approach might you take to interview transcription?

3. How might you go about qualitative data analysis?

4. Are there software programs for data management available for you to use, and might you test them out?

5. What might you employ to sense-check the categories of description as they begin to emerge?

6

Presenting the findings of phenomenographic work

In Chapter 5 we discussed and illustrated how, through the highly iterative analytical process associated with phenomenographic work, categories of description are surfaced. They were developed from the identification, sorting and resorting of 'utterances' and 'pools of meanings' (Åkerlind 2005d) which the focus shifts from the individual to the collective, given that '… treated collectively for the purposes of analysis, such that the focus is on the variations in understanding across the whole sample, rather than on the characteristics of individuals' responses' (Tight 2016: 320).

In this section of the book we discuss and illustrate the development of the outcome space, the method used to present aspects of described experiences: a visual representation of the categories of description, with the dimensions arranged in relation to one another. In particular, how

> the qualitatively different descriptions that emerge through phenomenographic analysis are logically related in terms of referential and structural aspects. In phenomenographic work, experience is discussed in terms of awareness and context; meaning that nothing is or can be experienced in isolation of both the structural aspect contains internal and external dimensions; the external dimension relates to context and the internal to awareness; with the referential aspect relating to the focus of awareness found to be

uppermost in the subject's account. (Taylor-Beswick 2019: 141–142)

Throughout the development of the categories of description, attention is paid to the relationship between the categories. The development of the outcome space is a discrete phase of phenomenographic research work within which the articulation of the referential and structural aspects of experience become even more pertinent. It is for this reason we offer this as a discrete chapter in this work. The outcome space is the means to offer findings to a range of audiences in a way that provides access to learning about experience on a theoretical and logical level.

Criteria for assessing the quality of the outcome space, which help to ensure robustness, were offered by Marton and Booth (1997: 125): each category should convey a distinctive way of understanding a phenomenon; categories are logically related; and the critical variation in the data was represented in as few categories as feasible. These benchmarks, in particular the pursuit of parsimony, include one of the more fixed and consistent practices seen across the phenomenographic literature (Figure 6.1). Relevant to this, as stated by Åkerlind (2005d: 323), is that 'ideally, the outcomes represent the full range of possible ways

Figure 6.1: Outcome space

Structural aspects	Referential aspects		
	Navigating the digital	Examining the digital	Reimagining the digital
DIGITAL EXPOSURE — Technical orientation — Professional orientation — Practice orientation	1. Expectations of the course 2. Being on the course	2. Being on the course 3. Observing others on the course	4. Applying learning to the course

Source: Taylor-Beswick (2019: 144)

of experiencing the phenomenon in question, at this particular point in time, for the population represented by the sample group collectively'.

Given the layers to constructing an outcome space, or outcome spaces, and the visuality associated with this, we include a range of examples, and signpost to notable studies or pieces of work that we have found helpful in respect of this particular phenomenographic practice. We begin with the following verbatim articulation of the process that was engaged in to work out and get to the outcome space:

> [R]elating to the analytical process that was carried out: accounts of experiences were grouped and regrouped into pools of meaning and from within these categories of description were identified, stabilised, and settled upon (Åkerlind, 2005b). Throughout what was an extensively iterative process, relationships between the categories of description were examined and re-examined, until a 'logically consistent' outcome space was formed (Ashwin, 2005, p.634). From within the pools of meaning four qualitative differences in the ways that digital development was described to have been experienced were identified. Categories were found to be more relational than hierarchically inclusive, but more importantly they are presented to reflect, as closely as possible, the world as it appeared to this student group. (Taylor-Beswick 2019: 80)

The categories of description (Box 6.1) and outcome space (Figure 6.1) relevant to this doctoral work are offered here to demonstrate how these two methods are interconnected and interact, and how outcomes may be reached and presented.

Box 6.1: Categories of description

Digital development, for this group of social work students, involved:

1. the expectations of the course
2. being on the course

3. observing others on the course
4. applying learning to the course

Source: Taylor-Beswick (2019: 90)

In this, a further excerpt, what is made clear is how the processes involved in the development of the categories of description and outcome space are highly iterative, but also highly valuable when working to stay as true as possible to the experiences as described by participants:

> The distinctly different categories of description presented in the previous section of this work (Chapter 4.2) were formed by examining students' descriptions of their digital experiences. The relationships between the categories of description were examined as part of this intensely iterative process; a process that involved numerous 'ah ha' moments as Åkerlind et al. (2005, p.95) describe them. Approaching the analysis in this way allowed for a 'testing' of coherence, through searching for 'evidence that undermined the draft representations' found (Åkerlind et al., 2005, p.94). Moving between these two methods of analysis, whilst time consuming and complex, provided a degree of confidence in the categories of description that were eventually settled upon. Whilst it could be thought of as extreme, 'going through five, ten to fifteen versions of the categories of description is necessary' when engaged in phenomenographic work, as Åkerlind et al. go on to contend, it is impossible to 'read the transcripts once and write the final categories of description' (2005, p.94). (Taylor-Beswick 2019: 141)

While reading, note how 'aspects are dialectically intertwined and occur simultaneously when we experience something' (Marton and Booth 1997: 87).

What is also worth noting at this point is how it is,

argued amongst some Phenomenographers that categories of description should be hierarchical (Marton 1981; Marton 1994; Yates et al 2012), however what appears to be more important and valued within the literature, is that they are relational (Marton and Pang, 2008; Pang and Ki, 2016); that is they show how each links to the other, in a way that can inform a pedagogic approach (Webb 1997). (Taylor-Beswick 2019: 52)

Taylor-Beswick (2019) found that the categories in this work were both relational and hierarchical. For the complete textual analysis of this example see Taylor-Beswick (2019), where the author defined and delineated the relationship between and across the categories of description. Additionally, Taylor-Beswick outlined how this final outcome space was developed and how this study was underpinned by the thinking of other and more established phenomenographers, in particular by Tight (2016: 320), who explained how epistemologically, 'phenomenographers operate with the underlying assumption that, for any given phenomenon of interest, there are only a limited number of ways of perceiving, understanding, or experiencing it'.

In another practice example, we provide an overview of phenomenographic research where two different outcome spaces were developed: one accentuating variation within the dimensions; the other outlining the relationship between the categories of descriptions (Hornung 2010). This is a method as described by Daniel (2022: 684) with reference to Åkerlind that involves the use of:

> a framework of 'themes of expanding awareness' to characterise both the variation between categories and their structural inter-relationships. Themes of expanding awareness are dimensions of variation that run through all the categories of description, whereby each higher, more comprehensive, level of awareness corresponds to some new additional dimension of variation in the theme. This critical variation delineates the different categories of description.

For Åkerlind (2005d: 324) it was a method where 'a search for meaning, or variation in meaning, across interview transcripts ... is then supplemented by a search for structural relationships between meanings'. In Hornung's (2010) work, five categories of description (Box 6.2) and four dimensions of variation (Box 6.3) were surfaced and developed.

Box 6.2: Categories of description

Category 1: CPD [continuing professional development] is upskilling for the sake of the organisation/library service (service orientation)
Category 2: CPD is about developing as a professional librarian (LIS [library and information studies] profession orientation)
Category 3: CPD is helping you to do all the jobs a One Person Librarian does (OPL orientation)
Category 4: CPD is when you have learned something, and you want to do things in a better way when you come back (personal orientation)
Category 5: CPD is about your development as a human being (lifelong learning orientation).

Source: Hornung (2010: 164)

Box 6.3: Example overview of dimensions of variation

Dimension *'role'* – responsibility, motivation, and support
Dimension *'time'* – current job or career or life in general
Dimension *'style'* – formal or informal with examples
Dimension *'networking'* – type of networking, reasons for doing it.

Source: Hornung (2010: 165)

As noted in Chapter 5, given that the vast majority of phenomenographic researchers work alone, 'some authors argue for the importance of bringing in additional researchers during the analysis to encourage greater open-mindedness and awareness of alternative perspectives, as a way of improving the final outcome space' (Åkerlind 2005d: 328). In Hornung's (2010) case, the work was carried out by a sole researcher and during the initial period of analysis six dimensions of variation emerged:

- Dimension skills – focusing on what kind of skills were sought, that is, library and information skills, subject specific skills, other skills.
- Dimension style – formal or informal style.
- Dimension type – kind of activity, for example, training course, conference, online resources.
- Dimension time – for current job or long-term career focus or lifelong learning, and so on.
- Dimension networking – type of networking, the reasons for doing it, and so on.
- Dimension incentive/motivation – who is the motivating force behind it? Do they have support from the employer?

Standard across the literature is the assumption that the number of categories and dimensions will 'typically … be relatively small' and that 'four or five variants are commonly found' (Tight 2016: 2). Discussing these initial dimensions with the supervisor, they agreed that the 'skills' dimension was very weak and did not constitute a proper dimension as there was no real difference between the categories. All of them had all types of skills listed and there was no preference detectable in any of them. Furthermore, the 'type' could be integrated into the 'style' dimension, strengthening it by adding examples. The focus of attention here is altered between 'formal' and 'informal', with one of them being in the foreground and one in the background. The dimension 'time' had both an internal and an external horizon. The focus was on either now (current job) or later (career or life in general). Dimension 'incentive/motivation' became 'role', because it was felt that the core of this dimension was the role the librarian perceived to be playing in the organisation. This would have implications for the motivation to do CPD with incentives not always given externally.

To articulate the findings further, with more depth and clarity, a detailed depiction of the categories is often developed. The next step was to show the focus of each dimension as pertained to each category and the researcher realised that there was considerable variation. Looking at the 'role', for example, CPD centred almost solely on the needs of the organisation in category 1, whereas in category 5 the human being took centre stage. Hornung (2010) followed Bowden's (2005b: 167) model on 'structures of categories' and developed this outcome space (see Table 6.1).

The relations of the categories to each other were developed and depicted visually. Category 5 (lifelong learning orientation) was the most highly developed as it incorporated all other categories. CPD was both an intrinsic need and an external object. Its focus had a lifelong dimension. In categories 1 (service orientation) and 3 (OPL orientation) CPD was experienced as an external object that could be manipulated for work-related goals. Category 1 (service orientation) had both a short-term and a long-term focus, category 3 (OPL orientation), however, only a short-term focus. In category 2 (LIS profession orientation), CPD was also experienced as an external object, which could be employed for professional motives, but veered towards CPD as an intrinsic need. It had a more long-term focus (career-related). Category 4 (personal orientation) was somewhat split into two. Where an interest came first, CPD was more experienced as an intrinsic need helping the librarian to develop as a person. Where the CPD came first, it became an external object to be used for work-related purposes.

A way of highlighting how the categories 'are logically related, typically as a hierarchy of structurally inclusive relationships' (Marton and Booth 1997: 125) is shown in Table 6.2. Here the categories (identified by their number) are ordered in a matrix outlining their places when seen through lenses of increasing awareness of the importance of learning and of the role of the individual. The categories range from short-term focus and development of work-related goals to a lifelong and holistic focus on learning where undertaking CPD has become an intrinsic need.

Combining the two outcome spaces in this work helped to illustrate how the categories were hierarchically related to each other (Figure 6.2). For example, category 5 (lifelong learning) was the most holistic, representing the crown of the tree with two branches leading downwards. One arm consisted of category 1

Table 6.1: Outcome space 1

Categories of description

CPD is...

Dimensions of variation	Category 1 (Service orientation)	Category 2 (LIS profession orientation)	Category 3 (OPL orientation)	Category 4 (Personal orientation)	Category 5 (Lifelong learning orientation)
	Upskilling for the sake of the organisation/library service	Developing a professional librarian	Helping you to do all the jobs an OPL does	When you have learned something, and you want to do things in a better way when you come back	About your development as a human being
Role – who is in charge?	Librarian and management in charge; often only management	Librarian in charge; management often against/indifferent	Librarian in charge	Librarian in charge	Librarian as human being (lifelong and life wide view)
Role – support?	Financial support and time off	Often no financial support and no time off	Financial support and time off	Often no financial support nor time off	Own time and own money
Style	Formal and informal; formal strong	Formal and informal; informal strong, but accreditation important	Very much informal	Formal and informal	Formal and informal, both very strong
Time	Current job, less career focus	Career focus, less current job	Very much current job – pressing need	Current job, also career (but with a more personal focus)	Lifelong – both current and future career as well as personal life
Networking – reasons?	View to problem solving (service)	Being a professional	View to problem solving (OPL status)	Acts as trigger to do something different/differently	Condition of being human
Networking – with whom?	People in organisation and librarians	With peers	Peers and experts in organisation and beyond	More accidental, e.g. speaking to people at conferences	Everybody

Source: Hornung (2010: 219–220)

Table 6.2: Outcome space 2

Structural aspects →	→ Increasing awareness of importance of learning →	Lifelong focus		5	5	5
		Long-term focus			2	
		Both		1	4	4
		Short-term focus		3		
Referential aspects →			*Development of skills for…*	*Work-related goals*	*Belonging to a profession*	*Developing as a person*
				CPD is an external object		CPD is an intrinsic need
			→ Increasing awareness of responsibility/role as an individual →			

Source: Hornung (2010: 223)

Figure 6.2: Hierarchy of categories

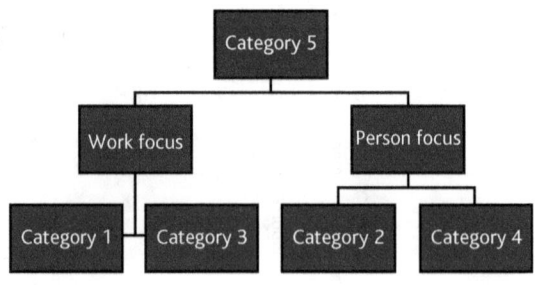

Source: Hornung (2010: 246)

(service orientation) and category 3 (OPL orientation) and had a work-centred purpose. The other branch had a person-centred focus and included category 2 (LIS profession orientation) and category 4 (personal orientation). It is worth noting that each interviewee could hold more than one conception in mind, or as explained it is 'not unusual to encounter fragments of two or three conceptions within the same interview' (Mimirinis and Ahlberg 2021: 572).

Throughout the literature the ways of presenting findings of qualitative research are wide and varied, and phenomenography is no exception. The approach taken is typically linked to the method, the targeted audience or readership, and what one is trying to convey in terms of a knowledge exchange or impact. For example, vignettes were constructed in one study to demonstrate how participants perceived the impact of the PhD on library services, which was one of the two research questions (Box 6.4). The findings had revealed three different conceptions for each of the two cohorts of interviewees (librarians and employers), but, unexpectedly, both sets of categories were quite similar. Additionally, the researcher discovered four dimensions of variations, which were identical for both groups, but with diverging priorities. The vignettes were composites, taking excerpts from the categories and dimensions of variations, interspersed with data collected from a focus group session. By creating hypothetical libraries and librarians, the researcher could illuminate the main points and different foci of each category.

Box 6.4: Use of vignettes

Vignette 1: The PhD as a means of transformation: growing future library services by elevating librarians and the LIS profession

In this library, the manager is very appreciative of having a librarian with a PhD. They may have actively recruited them and are interested in more staff enrolling in doctorates. They themselves are inspired to study again and comment on how much they have learned already. Often, they ask the PhD holder to do extra work at management level, including help setting policies or presenting data at an institutional level. There is a fear that other employees could see the PhD holder as the 'go to person' for the manager and that they could receive favours in return. For these employers, the doctorate helps combat stereotypes of libraries and librarians, which is reaching far beyond the organisation. The manager can see how PhDs can transform the profession. New avenues open for LIS, which will result in additional information services yet to be invented. Encouraging students and practitioners to pursue doctorates will help LIS strengthen its place among other academic subjects. Within the library, the person with the doctorate adds value to existing services. Their pedagogical knowledge allows them to evaluate the contribution of the library to academic processes and to suggest changes. The librarian has been involved in a wide range of library services: they offer outreach events on a grand scale, or they had been consulted on the new library building or cultural centre. Additionally, they have built partnerships with outside institutions. They have given presentations, published books and helped organise conferences. The librarian sees themselves as one of the gang and they usually do not mention their qualification. The colleagues appreciate having a librarian with a PhD in their midst as they are generous with the knowledge they gained through their studies.

Source: Hornung (2019: 60)

It is important to note that the vignettes did not constitute a single case study, but rather a meshing together of data derived from various informants aiming to make the rich data collected and the object of interest more accessible to readers (Reay et al 2019: 208). Vignettes are often used in ethnographic research as a way of giving attention to internal validity, and in phenomenographic research for the purposes explained by Lupton (2008: 42): 'it is important to balance the reductionist impression of the outcome space with vignettes that give some feeling of the flavours, scents and colours of human experience'. McKenzie (2003: 14) created vignettes in her phenomenographic PhD dissertation to highlight connections between different components of the results of the study.

Another method of presenting findings is through a graphic. The following example (Figure 6.3) is from Lupton's (2008: 139) PhD work, in the area of information literacy,

Figure 6.3: Outcome space

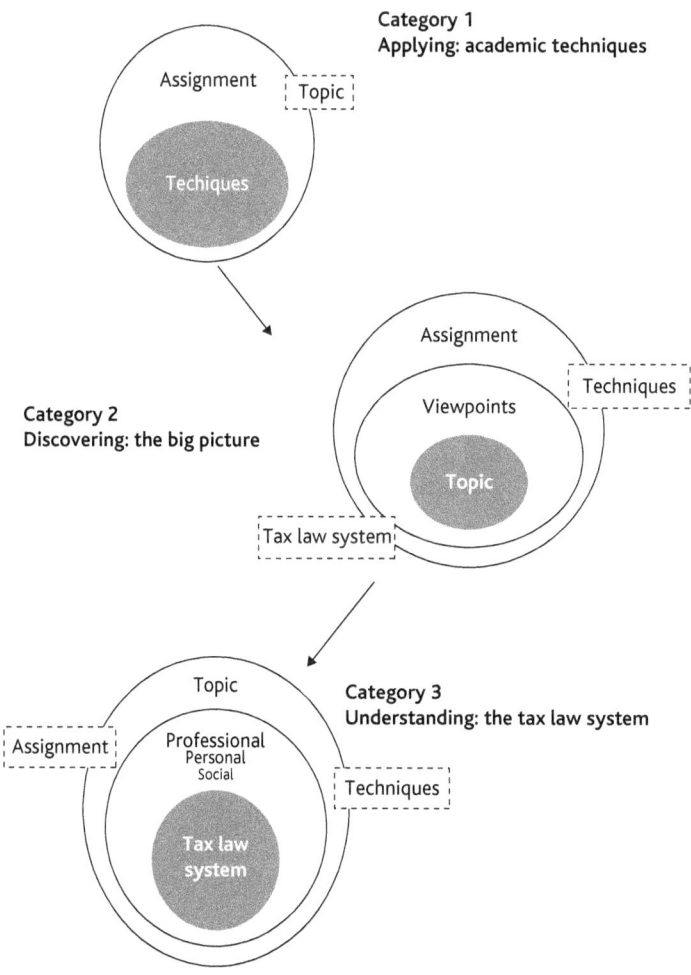

Source: Lupton (2008: 190)

where the outcome space was used to 'illustrate the qualitatively different ways that students experienced the relationship between information literacy and learning in the context of learning composition'.

Lupton (2008) also constructed an outcome space of the 'how' and 'what' of a conception (Figure 6.4) in line with Marton and Booth's (1997: 84–85) model, designed to examine conceptions.

Figure 6.4: 'How' and 'what' outcome space

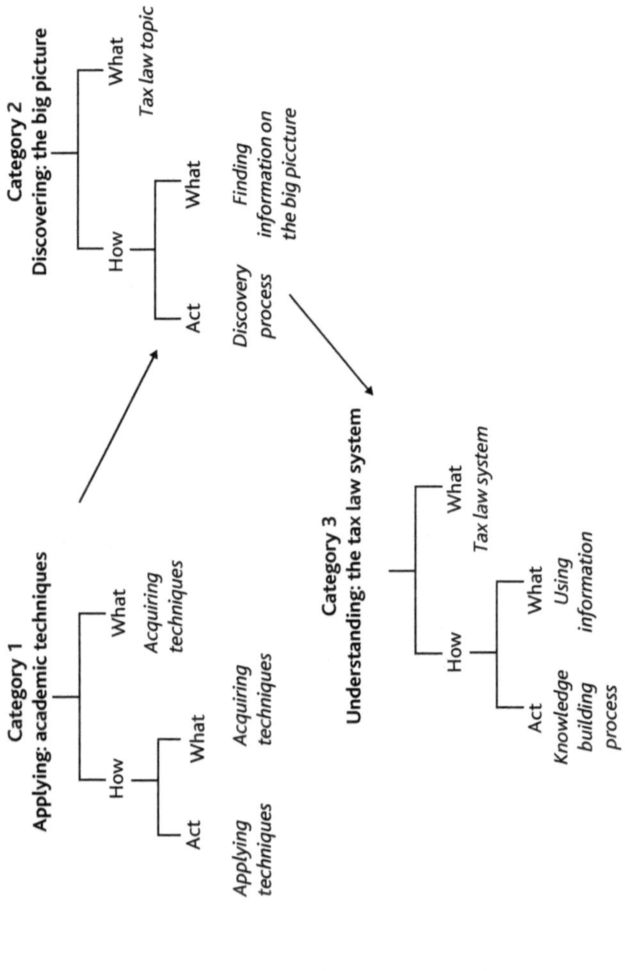

Source: Lupton (2008: 191)

As noted by Zhao (2015: 82/86), the 'what/how framework (Marton and Booth 1997), is a critical framework to analyse the basic unit in phenomenography – conception (Marton and Pong 2005), that represents 'the internal relationship between different conceptions ... analysed within a two-dimensional framework'.

Beagon (2021), on the other hand, created one outcome space in tabular form (Table 6.3) and one in pictorial form (Figure 6.5) for their PhD on academics' conceptions of professional skills.

It is helpful to engage with the rationale they offer for the approach taken:

> The final stage of the analysis results in an Outcome Space which describes all of the Categories of Description in relation to the Themes of Expanding Awareness. I began this process by creating a table showing the differences in each Category of Description with regard to each Theme of Expanding Awareness. The table morphed into the outcome spaces presented in tabular form. In creating the table, I found it helpful to consider the structural and referential framework (Harris, 2011). In this way, I considered that the Themes of Expanding Awareness were those aspects which described the structure of the phenomenon, the 'structural aspect' or the 'what'. When describing the categories, I used the concept of the referential framework, asking myself: 'How does each Category reference that structural aspect, what way is it referenced?' (Beagon 2021: 93–94)

As can be seen, there is much to be learnt from how phenomenographers work with and deploy phenomenographic methods and practices, and in particular how they arrive at, articulate, and present the findings of their work.

The essence of which is summarised brilliantly well by Rocha-Pinto et al, as:

> [D]efining and delimiting each conception identified in a phenomenographic study means describing

Table 6.3: Outcome space: conceptions of professional skills

Variation	Category A Communication	Category B Technical	Category C Enabling	Category D Combination	Category E Interpersonal	Category F Acting professionally
Purpose	To be able to **communicate verbally and in written form and to make your voice heard**	To have discipline-specific technical skills which you can **use as an engineer**	To enable a person **to be successful as** an engineer	To have a mix of technical and other skills **to function as** an engineer	To be able to **work with other people**, to have good relationships with your peers	To **act in a professional manner,** towards people and society
Benefit	Personal benefit	Industry benefit	Personal benefit	Personal and industry benefit	Personal and industry benefit	Personal, industry and societal benefit
Type	Non discipline-specific SKILLS Verbal and written communication	Discipline-specific technical SKILLS Technical Discipline Specific Skills	Non discipline-specific SKILLS Communication, present an argument, solve problems	Discipline-specific and non discipline-specific SKILLS Combination of skills	Non discipline-specific BEHAVIOUR Attitude towards others, respect and courtesy	Non discipline-specific SKILLS and BEHAVIOUR Attitude, responsibility, ethics & integrity

Source: Beagon and Bowe (2023: 1125)

the structural elements of the conceptions and how these elements vary in each one of the conceptions. These elements are called 'explanatory dimensions' (Åkerlind, 2005). The findings of phenomenographic study are embodied in a theoretical scheme called 'outcome space' (Åkerlind, 2005; Bowden & Walsh, 2000), where the relationship between each of the conceptions and the dimensions about a phenomenon is consubstantiation. (Rocha-Pinto et al 2019: 389)

For learning more about how to present the findings of phenomenographic work, we also recommend using databases of open access theses, some of which are listed in the 'Additional Resources' section. Again, we stress, while there is no right or wrong way to present the findings of phenomenographic work, there is a need to ensure that the work is underpinned by the practices and processes fundamental to the approach and that the workings out are made explicit, are accessible, and make sense to the readership.

Figure 6.5: Outcome space: conceptions of professional skills in pictorial form

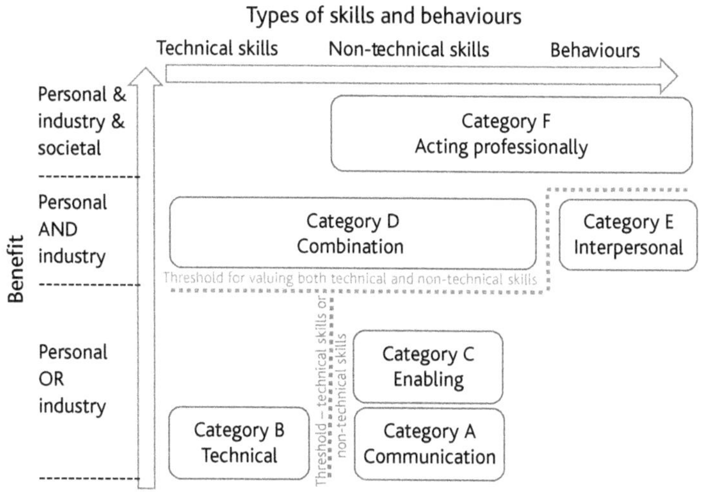

Source: Beagon and Bowe (2023: 1126).

Pause and reflect exercise

1. How might you sort, articulate and present the findings of your phenomenographic research?
2. Who is the target audience for your work?
3. What is your dissemination plan?
4. How will you know if your work has had an impact?

7

Conclusion

We conclude this book by drawing together the potentialities of the phenomenographic approach for researchers whose aim it is to describe and report on variation in experience of a particular phenomenon, including, but not limited to, those educational researchers with an interest in the development of 'instructional design' (Durden 2018: 21). We outline the impact of phenomenography work on policy and practice changes, and encourage further dialogue with us, our work and this book, and advocate engagement to learn more about the approach and connect with the active and vibrant phenomenography research community.

But before we do, a brief reminder of the journey that we, and hopefully the reader, have been on through the reading of this book. In Chapter 1, we provided our rationale for the why and why now of phenomenography, including an introduction to its origins, its actors, and its key protagonists. In Chapter 2, we traced the origins of phenomenographic research and worked to untangle key concepts and terminology. In Chapter 3, we introduced the main features of a phenomenographic research project, and the ways of assuring the robustness of the design, including the ethical implications. In Chapter 4, we took on the data generation methods associated with phenomenographic research, exemplified in the form of semi-structured interviews, and the possible involvement of a trigger, spark or related activity that serves to bring the phenomena of interest into focus. In Chapter 5, we offered examples of how to do and engage in the rigorous data analysis process associated with phenomenography, using our own doctoral work, and the work of others, to illustrate the steps involved. Finally, in Chapter 6, we provided an overview of how to present the results of a phenomenographic study with lots of visual references to support you to design and develop your own outcome space.

We now pause briefly to ponder the way forward for this research tradition, drawing on work and thinking linked to the origins of the approach, from within higher education. Wright and Osman (2018) proposed that phenomenography and variation theory as pedagogical frameworks have the power to transform teaching and learning. They posited that students and teachers would become aware that there are different understandings of one phenomenon arising from different worldviews, values and experiences, making the learning experience more inclusive and democratic. For Svensson (2016: 283), 'the focus in phenomenographic research on teachers and students as actors, and on their dealing with subject matter, is an especially promising development'. We can vouch that adopting a phenomenographic mindset makes better teachers by combining a first-order perspective with a second-order one:

- We have to find out the extent to which learners have progressed toward the competence that the teaching aims to develop
- To be able to develop that competence through teaching, we have to find out why some learners have been more successful than others in making such progress. (Marton and Booth 1997: 119)

An article by Rovio-Johansson and Ingerman (2016: 265) posed two questions about the possible future of phenomenographic research: 'Is phenomenography complete and finalised with no further development necessary?' and 'Is phenomenography relatively insignificant in the future development of the tradition as it has been transcended by variation theory?' In response, Åkerlind laid out the future for the approach, as she sees it:

> Of course, innovations in phenomenographic theory and methodology have continued since 2005, led

> especially by the large number of doctoral candidates using the research approach for their dissertations. However, it is clearly time for another book on phenomenographic research. A possible focus could be to highlight the methodological innovations being created by doctoral candidates, by undertaking a systematic search through phenomenographic theses.
> (Åkerlind 2018: 949)

We would not be so arrogant or presumptuous to suggest that this is that very book, but we are confident that we have reflected the work and innovations of phenomenography and laid the foundations for all of us to progress our abilities and confidence to develop the approach. And it is this that Rovio-Johansson and Ingerman (2016: 268) were supportive of and called for: 'it is reassuring that current activities indicate a committed community working in the tradition, continuing to develop it. Now, we invite the constructive and critical discussion of the tradition to continue'. Relating to this, as outlined by Entwistle (1997), is how the debates taking place within the phenomenographic community are part of a culture of academic debate and are a sign of impact. It is only through arguing, defending and explaining our stance that the approach can move forward. We hope that our book contributes to widening the ongoing debates and discussions, and that it brings phenomenography to new audiences in education and the world far beyond.

Considering the impact phenomenography has made on our own academic and professional endeavours, we can attest to its great value. In Amanda's case, phenomenography has shaped her teaching. It influenced changes to the curriculum for social workers in England and Northern Ireland, and she is currently working with Welsh colleagues to embed digital development into the training of social workers to ensure they are digitally informed and equipped. Eva has gained a new insight into her own learning and that of other people. She has introduced phenomenography to teachers frequenting her library who were looking for help with their research projects. This in turn has sparked spin-off events, for example, researcher symposia where those engaged in postgraduate work introduce their projects to colleagues in other centres and colleges. This renewed focus on evidence-based practice combined with her work on the research advisory group will influence the future direction and policies of her organisation. Other researchers reported similar policy and pedagogical implications arising from their phenomenographic PhD work. Kettunen (2017) emphasised how career practitioners benefited from reflecting on their own practice and becoming aware of how their own conceptions varied from those of others. The conceptions which became evident in their study showed that competencies were not only linked to new skills, but also to social, emotional and ethical factors. This in turn could improve their teaching if they provided learning experiences which factored in students' practical and conceptional understandings (Kettunen 2017: 50).

Finally, another phenomenographer, whose work we repeatedly return to, Entwistle, whose contributions to the field have held us in moments of confusion or apprehension; offered here for when you might need held or convincing and or for when one might begin to teach others about, and how *to do*, phenomenographic work:

> When introducing the idea of differing conceptions to students, I often ask them to explain the meaning of a word like 'antidote'. The students all know what the word means but have some difficulty in arriving at an agreed description of it. They often start with an example of having to give an antidote for a snake bite to exemplify its meaning, and then from other instances build up a more complete description. They soon realise that we do not store definitions in memory, but rather that the meaning resides within the interconnections of remembered instances and has to be reconstituted in providing an explanation. Moving from a relatively straightforward concept to a more problematic one, like 'justice', immediately demonstrates the somewhat idiosyncratic way in which we each understand abstract ideas. Phenomenography seeks to explore these different conceptions, or structures of awareness (Marton & Booth, 1997),

which people constitute from the world of their experience. (Entwistle 1997: 127)

It is our hope that for every person that leafs through the pages of this book, we will have another phenomenographer in the field, learning and reporting on how people experience phenomena in and of this world. This will help to develop the world in ways that we all can individually and collectively better exist. This is what we believe phenomenography and phenomenographers have to offer. As Ashworth and Lucas (2000: 300) wrote over 20 years ago, 'phenomenography is a methodology which has been quietly influential in research on higher education'. For us and for many others it certainly has.

Additional resources

Annotated bibliography
C.S. Bruce, H. Klaus and I.D. Stoodley (1998) have compiled a comprehensive annotated bibliography of phenomenographic research articles and books. This is a good introduction to some of the earlier core texts: https://eprints.qut.edu.au/42048/1/PhenomenographyBibliography2011.pdf

Databases
The following databases contain references to relevant doctoral theses:

- British Library's e-theses online service (EThOS): https://ethos.bl.uk/
- DART-Europe E-theses Portal gives global access to European research theses: https://www.dart-europe.org/
- Database of African Theses and Dissertations and Research (DATAD-R): https://datad.aau.org/
- EBSCO Open Dissertations: https://biblioboard.com/opendissertations/
- Open Access Theses and Dissertations: https://oatd.org/
- Networked Digital Library of Theses and Dissertations (NDLTD): http://search.ndltd.org/index.php
- ProQuest Dissertations & Theses Global: this resource is behind a paywall; you might have access to this resource through the library at your university: https://about.proquest.com/en/products-services/pqdtglobal/
- Trove (National Library of Australia): https://trove.nla.gov.au/landing/explore
- WorldCat: this database allows you to check which university library owns a thesis: https://www.worldcat.org/

Further reading: some recommended PhDs

Cope, C. (2000) *Educationally Critical Aspects of the Experience of Learning about the Concept of an Information System*, unpublished thesis (PhD), La Trobe University.

Cunningham, V. (2017) *Only Connect: A Phenomenographic Study Exploring Stakeholders' Conceptions of Information Literacy across an International Middle School Community*, unpublished thesis (DInfSci), Robert Gordon University, available at https://rgu-repository.worktribe.com/OutputFile/297122

Cutajar, M. (2014) *Post-Compulsory Pre-University Maltese Students' Accounts of their Networked Learning Experiences*, unpublished thesis (PhD), Lancaster University, available at https://eprints.lancs.ac.uk/id/eprint/72904/1/2014Cutajarphd.pdf

Forster, M. (2015) *An Investigation into Information Literacy in Nursing Practice: How Is It Experienced, What Are Its Parameters, and How Can It Be Developed?*, unpublished thesis (PhD), University of West London, available at https://repository.uwl.ac.uk/id/eprint/1271/1/Marc_Forster_Final_Thesis_(May_2015).pdf

Lupton, M. (2008) *Information Literacy and Learning*, unpublished thesis (PhD), Queensland University of Technology, available at https://eprints.qut.edu.au/16665/1/Mandy_Lupton_Thesis.pdf

McCracken, J. (2002) *Phenomenographic Instructional Design: Case Studies in Geological Mapping and Materials Science*, unpublished thesis (PhD), The Open University, available at https://oro.open.ac.uk/59388/1/270015.pdf

Wihlborg, M. (2005) *A Pedagogical Stance on Internationalising Education: An Empirical Study of Swedish Nurse Education from the Perspectives of Students and Teachers*, unpublished thesis (PhD), Lund University, available at https://typeset.io/pdf/a-pedagogical-stance-on-internationalising-education-an-1f8chof01w.pdf

References

Åkerlind, G. (2005a) 'Learning about phenomenography: Interviewing, data analysis and the qualitative research paradigm', in J.A. Bowden and P. Green (eds) *Doing Developmental Phenomenography*, Melbourne: RMIT Publishing, pp 63–73.

Åkerlind, G. (2005b) 'Phenomenographic methods: A case illustration', in J.A. Bowden and P. Green (eds) *Doing Developmental Phenomenography*, Melbourne: RMIT Publishing, pp 103–127.

Åkerlind, G. (2005c) 'Interim stages of the analysis of ways of experiencing being a university researcher', in J.A. Bowden and P. Green (eds) *Doing Developmental Phenomenography*, Melbourne: RMIT Publishing, pp 171–177.

Åkerlind, G.S. (2005d) 'Variation and commonality in phenomenographic research methods', *Higher Education Research & Development*, 24(4): 321–334. DOI: 10.1080/07294360500284672

Åkerlind, G.S. (2007) 'Constraints on academics' potential for developing as a teacher', *Studies in Higher Education*, 32(1): 21–37. DOI: 10.1080/03075070601099416

Åkerlind, G.S. (2008) 'A phenomenographic approach to developing academics' understanding of the nature of teaching and learning', *Teaching in Higher Education*, 13(6): 633–644. DOI: 10.1080/13562510802452350

Åkerlind, G.S. (2012) 'Variation and commonality in phenomenographic research methods', *Higher Education Research & Development*, 31(1): 115–127. DOI: 10.1080/07294360.2011.642845

Åkerlind, G.S. (2015) 'From phenomenography to variation theory: A review of the development of the variation theory of learning and implications for pedagogical design in higher education', *HERDSA Review of Higher Education*, 2: 5–26, available at https://www.herdsa.org.au/herdsa-review-higher-education-vol-2/5–26

Åkerlind, G.S. (2018) 'What future for phenomenographic research? On continuity and development in the phenomenography and variation theory research tradition', *Scandinavian Journal of Educational Research*, 62(6): 949–958. DOI: 10.1080/00313831.2017.1324899

Åkerlind, G.S. (2022) 'Critique of the article, "Theoretical foundations of phenomenography: a critical review"', *Higher Education Research & Development*, 42(6): 1299–1308. DOI: 10.1080/07294360.2022.2142535

Åkerlind, G.S., Bowden, J. and Green, P. (2005) 'Learning to do phenomenography: A reflective discussion', in J.A. Bowden and P. Green (eds) *Doing Developmental Phenomenography*, Melbourne: RMIT Publishing, pp 74–100.

Alsop, G. and Tompsett, C. (2006) 'Making sense of "pure" phenomenography in information and communication technology in education', *Research in Learning Technology*, 14(3): 241–259. DOI: 10.1080/09687760600837058

Andretta, S. (2007) 'Phenomenography: A conceptual framework for information literacy education', *Aslib Proceedings: New Information Perspectives*, 59(2): 152–168. DOI: 10.1108/00012530710736663

Ashwin, P. (2005) 'Variation in students' experiences of the "Oxford Tutorial"', *Higher Education*, 50(4): 631–644. DOI: 10.1007/s10734-004-6369-6

Ashwin, P., Boud, D., Coate, K., Hallett, F., Keane, E., Krause, K.-L., Leibowitz, B., MacLaren, I., McArthur, J., McCune, V. and Tooher, M. (2015) *Reflective Teaching in Higher Education*, London: Bloomsbury.

Ashworth, P. and Lucas, U. (2000) 'Achieving empathy and engagement: A practical approach to the design, conduct and reporting of phenomenographic research', *Studies in Higher Education*, 25(3): 295–308. DOI: 10.1080/713696153

Babbie, E. (2016) *The Basics of Social Research*, seventh edition, Boston: Cengage Learning.

Barnard, A., McCosker, H. and Gerber, R. (1999) 'Phenomenography: A qualitative research approach for exploring understanding in health care', *Qualitative Health Research*, 9(2): 212–226. DOI: 10.1177/104973299129121794

References

Barrow, J.M., Brannan, G.D. and Khandhar, P.B. (2022) 'Research ethics', in StatPearls [Internet]. Treasure Island (FL): StatPearls Publishing; 2023 Jan–. PMID: 29083578, available at https://www.statpearls.com/point-of-care/34721

Baughan, P. (2019) *'The Sociological Imagination': Researching Sustainability, using Phenomenography*, unpublished thesis (PhD), Lancaster University, available at https://eprints.lancs.ac.uk/id/eprint/154664/1/2019baughanphd.pdf

Beagon, U. (2021) *A Phenomenographic Study of Academics Teaching on Engineering Programmes in Ireland: Conceptions of Professional Skills and Approaches to Teaching Professional Skills*, unpublished thesis (PhD), TU Dublin, available at https://arrow.tudublin.ie/engdoc/125/

Beagon, U. and Bowe, B. (2023) 'Understanding professional skills in engineering education: A phenomenographic study of faculty conceptions', *Journal of Engineering Education*, 112(4): 1109–1144. DOI: 10.1002/jee.20556

Beaulieu, R. (2017) 'Phenomenography: Implications for expanding the educational action research lens', *Canadian Journal of Action Research*, 18(2): 62–81. DOI: 10.33524/cjar.v18i2.335

Belluigi, D.Z. and Taylor-Beswick, A. (2022) 'At the interstices of ethics, the digital & research in higher education', *BERA Research Intelligence*, 151: 38–39.

Biggs, J.B. (2003) *Teaching for Quality Learning at University: What the Student Does*, second edition, Maidenhead: Society for Research into Higher Education & Open University Press.

Boon, S., Johnston, B. and Webber, S. (2007) 'A phenomenographic study of English faculty's conceptions of information literacy', *Journal of Documentation*, 62(2): 204–228. DOI: 10.1108/00220410710737187

Booth, S. (1997) 'On phenomenography, learning and teaching', *Higher Education Research & Development*, 16(2): 135–158. DOI: 10.1080/0729436970160203

Blair, E. (2017) *Hearing the Student Voice: Finding Value in Feedback*, [online] 4 May, available at https://www.researchgate.net/publication/323629543_Hearing_the_student_voice_finding_value_in_feedback

Bokhove, C. and Downey, C. (2018) 'Automated generation of "good enough" transcripts as a first step to transcription of audio-recorded data', *Methodological Innovations*, 11(2): 1–14. DOI: 10.1177/2059799118790743

Bowden, J.A. (2000) 'The nature of phenomenographic research', in J.A. Bowden and E. Walsh (eds) *Phenomenography*, Melbourne: RMIT Publishing, pp 1–18.

Bowden, J.A. (2005a) 'Reflections on the phenomenographic team research process', in J.A. Bowden and P. Green (eds) *Doing Developmental Phenomenography*, Melbourne: RMIT Publishing, pp 11–31.

Bowden, J.A. (2005b) 'Records of iterative processes in reaching version 8 of the "success" categories of description', in J.A. Bowden and P. Green (eds) *Doing Developmental Phenomenography*, Melbourne: RMIT Publishing, pp 156–170.

Bowden, J.A. and Green, P. (eds) (2005) *Doing Developmental Phenomenography*, Melbourne: RMIT University Press.

Bowden, J.A. and Green, P.J. (2019) *Playing the PhD Game with Integrity: Connecting Research, Professional Practice and Educational Context*, Singapore: Springer Nature.

Bowden, J.A. and Marton, F. (2004) *The University of Learning: Beyond Quality and Competence*, London and New York: Routledge Falmer.

Bowden, J.A. and Walsh, E. (eds) (2000) *Phenomenography*, Melbourne: RMIT University Press.

Bowden, J.A., Green, P., Barnacle, R., Cherry, N. and Usher, R. (2005) 'Academics' ways of understanding success in research activities', in J.A. Bowden and P. Green (eds) *Doing Developmental Phenomenography*, Melbourne: RMIT Publishing, pp 128–144.

Brinkmann, S. and Kvale, S. (2015) *InterViews: Learning the Craft of the Qualitative Research Interviewing*, third edition, Los Angeles: SAGE.

Bruce, C.S. (1997) *The Seven Faces of Information Literacy*, Adelaide: Auslib Press.

Bruce, C.S. (1998) 'The phenomenon of information literacy', *Higher Education Research & Development*, 17(1): 25–43. DOI: 10.1080/0729436980170102

References

Bruce, C.S. (1999) 'Phenomenography: Opening a new territory for library and information science research', *The New Review of Information and Library Research*, 5(1): 31–47, available at https://eprints.qut.edu.au/57651/1/57651.pdf

Bruce, C.S. and Stoodley, I.D. (2013) 'Experiencing higher degree research supervision as teaching', *Studies in Higher Education*, 38(2): 226–241. DOI: 10.1080/03075079.2011.576338

Bruce, C.S., Klaus, H. and Stoodley, I. (1998) 'An annotated bibliography of phenomenographic research: Selected publications to 1997', Brisbane: Queensland University of Technology, available at https://eprints.qut.edu.au/42048/1/PhenomenographyBibliography2011.pdf

Bruce, C., Buckingham, L., Hynd, J., Mcmahon, C., Roggenkamp, M. and Stoodley, I. (2004) 'Ways of experiencing the act of learning to program: A phenomenographic study of introductory programming students at university', *Journal of Information Technology Education*, 3: 143–160. DOI: 10.28945/294

Cibangu, S.K. and Hepworth, M. (2016) 'The uses of phenomenology and phenomenography: A critical review', *Library & Information Science Research*, 38(2): 148–160. DOI: 10.1016/j.lisr.2016.05.001

Cohen, L., Manion, L. and Morrison, K. (2017) *Research Methods in Education*, eighth edition, London and New York: Routledge.

Collier-Reed, B.J. and Ingerman, Å. (2013) 'Phenomenography: From critical aspects to knowledge claim', in M. Tight and J. Huisman (eds) *Theory and Method in Higher Education Research*, Bingley: Emerald Publishing Limited, pp 243–260.

Collier-Reed, B.J., Ingerman, Å. and Berglund, A. (2009) 'Reflections on trustworthiness in phenomenographic research: Recognising purpose, context and change in the process of research', *Education as Change*, 13(2): 339–355. DOI: 10.1080/16823200903234901

Collin, K. (2006) 'Connecting work and learning: Design engineers' learning at work', *Journal of Workplace Learning*, 18(7/8): 403–413. DOI: 10.1108/13665620610692971

Cope, C. (2004) 'Ensuring validity and reliability in phenomenographic research using the analytical framework of a structure of awareness', *Qualitative Research Journal*, 4(2): 4–18.

Cossham, A.F. (2017) 'An evaluation of phenomenography', *Library and Information Research*, 41(125): 17–31. DOI: 10.29173/lirg755

Cresswell, J.W. (2022) *Research Design: Qualitative, Quantitative, and Mixed Methods Approaches*, sixth edition, Los Angeles: SAGE.

Cresswell, J.W. and Cresswell, J.D. (2018) *Research Design: Qualitative, Quantitative, and Mixed Methods Approaches*, fifth edition, Thousand Oaks: SAGE.

Dahlgren, L.O. and Fallsberg, M. (1991) 'Phenomenography as a qualitative approach in social pharmacy research', *Journal of Social and Administrative Pharmacy*, 8(4): 150–156.

Dahlgren, L.O. and Marton, F. (1978) 'Students' conceptions of subject matter: an aspect of learning and teaching in higher education', *Studies in Higher Education*, 3(1): 25–35. DOI: 10.1080/03075077812331376316

Dahlin, B. (2007) 'Enriching the theoretical horizons of phenomenography, variation theory and learning studies', *Scandinavian Journal of Educational Research*, 51(4): 327–346. DOI: 10.1080/00313830701485437

Daniel, S. (2022) 'A phenomenographic outcome space for ways of experiencing lecturing', *Higher Education Research & Development*, 41 (3): 681–698. DOI: 10.1080/07294360.2021.1872055

Davis, M.B. (2007) *Doing a Successful Research Project: Using Qualitative or Quantitative Methods*, Basingstoke and New York: Palgrave Macmillan.

Davis, P., Ingerman, A. and Kettunen, J. (2019) *EARLI, SIG 9 Phenomenography and Variation Theory Newsletter*, available at https://ssl.earli.org/sites/default/files/2019-03/SIG%209newsletter_spring2019.pdf

Denholm, C. (2023) *What Do We Mean by Innovative Teaching? A Phenomenographic Study of Academics' Perspectives*, unpublished thesis (PhD), University of the West of England, available at https://uwe-repository.worktribe.com/OutputFile/10441451

de Villiers, C., Farooq, M.B. and Molinari, M. (2022) 'Qualitative research interviews using online video technology – challenges and opportunities', *Meditari Accountancy Research*, 30(6): 1764–1782. DOI: 10.1108/MEDAR-03-2021-1252

References

Doucet, A. and Mauthner, N. (2008) 'Qualitative interviewing and feminist research', in J. Brannen, P. Alasuutari and L. Bickman (eds) *The SAGE Handbook of Social Research Methods*, London: SAGE, pp 328–343.

Dringenberg, E., Mendoza-Garcia, J.A., Tafur, M., Fila, N.D. and Hsu, M.C. (2015) 'Using phenomenography: Reflections on key considerations for making methodological decisions', in *2015 ASEE Annual Conference & Exposition, June 14–17, 2015*, Seattle, Washington, Paper ID #11839, available at https://peer.asee.org/using-phenomenography-reflections-on-key-considerations-for-making-methodological-decisions.pdf

Duncombe, J. and Jessop, J. (2012) '"Doing rapport" and the ethics of "faking friendship"', in T. Miller, M. Birch, M. Mauthner and J. Jessop (eds) *Ethics in Qualitative Research*, second edition, Los Angeles: SAGE, pp 108–121.

Dunkin, R. (2000) 'Using phenomenography to study organisational change', in J.A. Bowden and E. Walsh (eds) *Phenomenography*, Melbourne: RMIT University Press, pp 137–152.

Durden, G. (2016) *An Investigation into Beginner Teachers' Knowledge and Learning Study*, unpublished thesis (PhD), University of Birmingham, available at https://etheses.bham.ac.uk//id/eprint/6754/1/Durden16PhD.pdf

Durden, G. (2018) 'Accounting for the context in phenomenography-variation theory: Evidence of English graduates' conceptions of price', *International Journal of Educational Research*, 87: 12–21. DOI: 10.1016/j.ijer.2017.11.005

EARLI (European Association for Research on Learning and Instruction) (2023) *Special Interest Group SIG 9, Phenomenography and Variation Theory*, available at https://www.earli.org/sig/sig-9-phenomenography-and-variation-theory

Edwards, S.L. (2007) 'Phenomenography: "Follow the yellow brick road"!', in S. Lipu, K. Williamson and A. Lloyd (eds) *Exploring Methods in Information Literacy Research*, Oxford: Chandos Publishing, pp 87–106.

Egan, G. (2017) *The Skilled Helper*, second edition, Andover: Cengage Learning EMEA.

Ellis, C. (2007) 'Telling secrets, revealing lives: Relational ethics in research with intimate others', *Qualitative Inquiry*, 13(1): 3–29. DOI: 10.1177/1077800406294947

Entwistle, N. (1997) 'Introduction: Phenomenography in higher education', *Higher Education Research & Development*, 16(2): 127–134. DOI: 10.1080/0729436970160202

Entwistle, N. (2018) *Student Learning and Academic Understanding: A Research Perspective with Implications for Teaching*, Cambridge, MA: Elsevier Academic Press.

Esterberg, K.G. (2002) *Qualitative Methods in Social Research*, Boston: McGraw Hill.

Fawns, T., Ross, J., Carbonel, H., Noteboom, J., Finnegan-Dehn, S. and Raver, M. (2023) 'Mapping and tracing the postdigital: Approaches and parameters of postdigital research', *Postdigital Science and Education*, 5(3): 623–642. DOI: 10.1007/s42438-023-00391-y

Fázik, J. and Steinerová, J. (2021) 'Technologies, knowledge and truth: The three dimensions of information literacy of university students in Slovakia', *Journal of Documentation*, 77(1): 285–303. DOI: 10.1108/JD-05-2020-008

Feldon, D.F. and Tofel-Grehl, C. (2022) 'Phenomenography as a basis for fully integrated mixed methodologies', in J.H. Hitchcock and A.J. Onwuegbuzie (eds) *The Routledge Handbook for Advancing Integration in Mixed Methods Research*, Abingdon: Routledge, pp 23–56.

Forster, M. (2016) 'Phenomenography: A methodology for information literacy research', *Journal of Librarianship and Information Science*, 48(4): 353–362. DOI: 10.1177/0961000614566481

Forster, M. (2018) '"Ethnographic" thematic phenomenography: A methodological adaptation for the study of information literacy in an ontologically complex workplace', *Journal of Documentation*, 75(2): 349–365. DOI: 10.1108/JD-05-2018-0079

Francis, H. (1996) 'Advancing phenomenography: Questions of methods', in G. Dall'Alba and B. Hasselgren (eds) *Reflections on Phenomenography: Toward a Methodology?*, Göteborg: Acta Universitatis Gothoburgensis, pp 35–48.

References

Gerber, R. (2001) 'The concept of common sense in workplace learning and experience', *Education and Training*, 43(2): 72–81. DOI: 10.1108/EUM0000000005424

Gibbs, G., Morgan, A. and Taylor, E. (1982) 'A review of the research of Ference Marton and the Goteborg Group: A phenomenological research perspective on learning', *Higher Education*, 11(2): 123–145. DOI: 10.1007/BF00139684

Go, L. and Pang, M.F. (2021) 'Phenomenography in the "lived" context of parental learning', *International Journal of Qualitative Methods*, 20: 1–10. DOI: 10.1177/16094069211016160

Goldkind, L., LaMendola, W. and Taylor-Beswick, A. (2020) 'Tackling COVID-19 is a crucible for privacy', *Journal of Technology in Human Services*, 38(2): 89–90. DOI: 10.1080/15228835.2020.1757559

Gorman, G.E. and Clayton, P. (2005) *Qualitative Research for the Information Professional: A Practical Handbook*, second edition, London: Facet Publishing.

Green, P. (2005) 'A rigorous journey into phenomenography: From the naturalistic inquirer standpoint', in J.A. Bowden and P. Green (eds) *Doing Developmental Phenomenography*, Melbourne: RMIT University Press, pp 32–46.

Green, P. and Bowden, J. (2009) 'Principles of developmental phenomenography', *Malaysian Journal of Qualitative Research*, 2(2): 52–70, available at https://www.qramalaysia.org/journals-vol2

Guba, E.G. and Lincoln, Y.S. (1989) *Fourth Generation Evaluation*, Newbury Park: SAGE.

Hallett, F. (2014) 'The dilemma of methodological idolatry in higher education research: The case of phenomenography', in J. Huisman and M. Tight (eds) *Theory and Method in Higher Education Research II*, Bingley: Emerald Group Publishing Limited, pp 203–225. DOI: 10.1108/S1479-3628(2014)0000010016

Halttunen, K. (2003) 'Students' conceptions of information retrieval: Implications for the design of learning environments', *Library & Information Science Research*, 25(3): 307–332. DOI: 10.1016/S0740-8188(03)00032-X

Han, F. and Ellis, R.A. (2019) 'Using phenomenography to tackle key challenges in science education', *Frontiers in Psychology*, 10: 1–10, article number 1414. DOI: 10.3389/fpsyg.2019.01414

Harris, L.R. (2011) 'Phenomenographic perspectives on the structure of conceptions: The origins, purposes, strengths, and limitations of the what/how and referential/structural frameworks', *Educational Research Review*, 6(2): 109–124. DOI: 10.1016/j.edurev.2011.01.002

Hasselgren, B. and Beach, D. (1997) 'Phenomenography: A "good-for nothing brother" of phenomenology? Outline of an analysis', *Higher Education Research & Development*, 16(2): 191–202. DOI: 10.1080/0729436970160206

Hessenauer, S. and Zastrow, Z. (2013) 'Becoming a social worker: BSW social workers' educational experiences', *Journal of Baccalaureate Social Work*, 18(1): 19–35. DOI: 10.18084/basw.18.1.lv0g0h687704211t

Holmes, A.G.D. (2020) 'Researcher positionality: A consideration of its influence and place in qualitative research – a new researcher guide', *Shanlax International Journal of Education*, 8(4): 1–10. DOI: 10.34293/education.v8i4.3232

Holmqvist, M. and Selin, P. (2019) 'What makes the difference? An empirical comparison of critical aspects identified in phenomenographic and variation theory analyses', *Palgrave Communications*, 5: article number 71. DOI: 10.1057/s41599-019-0284-z

Holstein, J.A. and Gubrium, J.F. (1995) *Qualitative Research Methods: The Active Interview*, Thousand Oaks: SAGE.

Hoover, R.S. and Koerber, A.L. (2009) 'Using NVivo to answer the challenges of qualitative research in professional communication: Benefits and best practices tutorial', *IEEE Transactions on Professional Communication*, 54(1): 68–82. DOI: 10.1109/TPC.2009.2036896

Hornung, E. (2010) *The Current State and Perceptions of One-Person Librarians in Ireland of Continuing Professional Development*, unpublished thesis (PhD), University of Sheffield.

Hornung, E. (2012) 'One-person librarians and continuing professional development: How the LAI can make a difference', *An Leabharlann*, 21(1): 15–19, available at https://www.libraryassociation.ie/wp-content/uploads/2018/11/Mar_12_Leabharlann_21_1.pdf

Hornung, E. (2019) *Do We Need a Doctor in the Library? Perceptions of Librarians and Managers in Ireland: A Phenomenographic Study*, unpublished thesis (M.Ed.), Trinity College Dublin, available at http://www.tara.tcd.ie/bitstream/handle/2262/92777/HornungSchEdu2020.pdf

Huntley, H. (2003) *Beginning Teachers' Conceptions of Competence*, unpublished thesis (Ed.D.), Central Queensland University, available at https://library-resources.cqu.edu.au/thesis/adt-QCQU/uploads/approved/adt-QCQU20050512.134448/public/01front.pdf

Israel, M. and Hay, I. (2006) *Research Ethics for Scientists: Between Ethical Conduct and Regulatory Compliance*, London: SAGE.

Jandrić, P., Knox, J., Besley, T., Ryberg, T., Suoranta, J. and Hayes, S. (2018) 'Postdigital science and education', *Educational Philosophy and Theory*, 50(10): 893–899. DOI: 10.1080/00131857.2018.1454000

Kara, H. (2012) *Research and Evaluation for Busy Practitioners: A Time Saving Guide*, Bristol: Policy Press.

Kara, H. (2018) *Research Ethics in the Real World: Euro-Western and Indigenous Perspectives*, Bristol: Policy Press.

Kara, H. (2020) *Creative Research Methods in Social Sciences: A Practical Guide*, second edition, Bristol: Policy Press.

Kara, H. (2022) *Qualitative Research for Quantitative Researchers*, Los Angeles: SAGE.

Kelly, P. (2002) 'Validity and discursive phenomenography', paper presented to the British Educational Research Association Conference, University of Exeter, September 2002.

Kettunen, J. (2017) *Career Practitioners' Conceptions of Social Media and Competency for Social Media in Career Services*, unpublished thesis (PhD), University in Jyväskylä, available at https://jyx.jyu.fi/bitstream/handle/123456789/55367/978-951-39-7160-1.pdf

Kettunen, J. and Tynjälä, P. (2018) 'Applying phenomenography in guidance and counselling research', *British Journal of Guidance & Counselling*, 46(1): 1–11. DOI: 10.1080/03069885.2017.1285006

Kiley, M. and Wisker, G. (2009) 'Threshold concepts in research education and evidence of threshold crossing', *Higher Education Research & Development*, 28(4): 431–441. DOI: 10.1080/07294360903067930

King, A. (1993) 'From sage on the stage to guide on the side', *College Teaching*, 41(1): 30–35, available at https://faculty.washington.edu/kate1/ewExternalFiles/SageOnTheStage.pdf

Kullberg, A. and Ingerman, Å. (2022) 'Researching conditions of learning: Phenomenography and variation theory', in *Oxford Research Encyclopaedia of Education*, Oxford: Oxford University Press. DOI: 10.1093/acrefore/9780190264093.013.1708

Kumar, R. (2019) *Research Methodology: A Step-by-Step Guide for Beginners*, fifth edition, Los Angeles: SAGE.

Kvale, S. (1996) *InterViews: An Introduction to Qualitative Research Interviewing*, Thousand Oaks: SAGE.

Lapadat, J.C. (2000). 'Problematizing transcription: Purpose, paradigm and quality', *International Journal of Social Research Methodology*, 3(3): 203–219. DOI: 10.1080/13645570050083698

Larsson, J. and Holmström, I. (2007) 'Phenomenographic or phenomenological analysis: Does it matter? Examples from a study on anaesthesiologists' work', *International Journal of Qualitative Studies on Health and Well-being*, 2(1): 55–64. DOI: 10.1080/17482620601068105

Leadbetter, D. and Bell, A. (2018) 'What can dental education gain by understanding student experience of the curriculum?', *European Journal of Dental Education*, 22(3): 468–478. DOI: 10.1111/eje.12327

Limberg, L. (1999) 'Experiencing information seeking and learning: A study of the interaction between two phenomena', *Information Research*, 5(1), available at http://informationr.net/ir/5-1/paper68.html

Limberg, L. (2000) 'Phenomenography: A relational approach to research on information needs, seeking and use', *New Review of Information Behaviour Research*, 1: 51–67.

Limberg, L. (2005) 'Phenomenography', in K.E. Fisher, S. Erdelez and L. McKechnie (eds) *Theories of Information Behavior*, Medford: Information Today, pp 280–283.

Lincoln, Y. and Guba, E.G. (1985) *Naturalistic Inquiry*, Beverly Hills: SAGE.

Ling, L.M. and Marton, F. (2012) 'Towards a science of the art of teaching: Using variation theory as a guiding principle of pedagogical design', *International Journal for Lesson and Learning Studies*, 1(1): 7–22. DOI: 10.1108/20468251211179678

Lister, P. (2022) 'Future–present learning and teaching: A case study in smart learning', in E. Sengupta and P. Blessinger (eds), *Changing the Conventional University Classroom*, Bingley: Emerald Publishing Limited, pp 61–79.

Lizier, A.L. (2022) 'Re-considering the nature of work in complex adaptive organisations: Fluid work as a driver of learning through work', *Journal of Workplace Learning*, 34(2): 150–161. DOI: 10.1108/JWL-09-2020-0152

Lo, M.L. (2012) *Variation Theory and the Improvement of Teaching and Learning*, Göteborg: Acta Universitatis Gothoburgensis, available at https://gupea.ub.gu.se/bitstream/handle/2077/29645/gupea_2077_29645_5.pdf?sequence=5

Lupton, M. (2008) *Information Literacy and Learning*, unpublished thesis (PhD), Queensland University of Technology, available at https://eprints.qut.edu.au/16665/1/Mandy_Lupton_Thesis.pdf

Marshall, C. and Rossman, G.B. (2006) *Designing Qualitative Research*, fourth edition, Thousand Oaks: SAGE.

Marshall, C. and Rossman, G.B. (2016) *Designing Qualitative Research*, sixth edition, Los Angeles: SAGE.

Martin, E. (2005) 'Introduction: Special issue in tribute to John Bowden', *Higher Education Research & Development*, 24(4): 287–291. DOI: 10.1080/07294360500284557

Marton, F. (1975) 'What does it take to learn?', in N.J. Entwistle and D. Hounsell (eds) *How Students Learn*, Lancaster: University of Lancaster. Reprinted as Marton, F. (2018) 'Appendix B3: What does it take to learn?', in N. Entwistle (ed) *Student Learning and Academic Understanding*, Cambridge, MA: Academic Press, pp 307–317.

Marton, F. (1976) 'What does it take to learn? Some implications of an alternative view of learning', in N. Entwistle (ed) *Strategies for Research and Development in Higher Education*, Amsterdam: Swets & Zeitlinger, pp 32–42.

Marton, F. (1979) 'Learning as seen from the learner's point of view', in H. Fritsch (ed) *Ziff Papiere*, 30, Hagen: Fern Universität Hagen, available at http://files.eric.ed.gov/fulltext/ED317156.pdf

Marton, F. (1981) 'Phenomenography: Describing conceptions of the world around us', *Instructional Science*, 10(2): 177–200. DOI: 10.1007/BF00132516

Marton, F. (1986) 'Phenomenography: A research approach to investigating different understandings of reality', *Journal of Thought*, 21(3): 28–49. DOI: https://www.jstor.org/stable/42589189

Marton, F. (1988) 'Phenomenography: Exploring different conceptions of reality', in D. Fetterman (ed) *Qualitative Approaches to Evaluation in Education: The Silent Scientific Revolution*, New York: Praeger, pp 176–205.

Marton, F. (1992) 'The experiential turn', *Current Contents*, 34: 8, available at https://garfield.library.upenn.edu/classics1992/A1992JH47000001.pdf

Marton, F. (1994) 'Phenomenography', in T. Husén and T.N. Postlethwaite (eds) *The International Encyclopedia of Education*, second edition, volume 8, Oxford: Pergamon, pp 4424–4429, available at https://edisciplinas.usp.br/pluginfile.php/6402696/mod_resource/content/0/Marton%20%281994%29.pdf

Marton, F. (2000) 'The structure of awareness', in J.A. Bowden and E. Walsh (eds) *Phenomenography*, Melbourne: RMIT University Press, pp 102–116.

Marton, F. (2015) *Necessary Conditions of Learning*, New York and London: Routledge.

Marton, F. (2018) 'Towards a pedagogical theory of learning', in K. Matsushita (ed) *Deep Active Learning Toward Greater Depth in University Education*, Singapore: Springer Nature, pp 59–77.

Marton, F. and Booth, S. (1997) *Learning and Awareness*, Mahwah: Lawrence Erlbaum Associates.

Marton, F. and Bowden, J. (1998) *The University of Learning: Beyond Quality and Competence in Higher Education*, London: Kogan Page.

Marton, F. and Neuman, D. (1996) 'Phenomenography and children's experience of division', in L.P. Steffe, P. Nesher, P. Cobb, B. Sriraman and B. Greer (eds) *Theories of Mathematical Learning*, Mahwah: Lawrence Erlbaum Associates Publishers, pp 315–334.

Marton, F. and Pang, M.F. (2006) 'On some necessary conditions of learning', *The Journal of Learning Sciences*, 15(2): 193–220. DOI: https://www.jstor.org/stable/25473516

Marton, F. and Pang, M.F. (2008) 'The idea of phenomenography and the pedagogy of conceptual change', in S. Vosniadou (ed) *International Handbook on Research of Conceptual Change*, New York and London: Routledge, pp 533–559.

References

Marton, F. and Pang, M.F. (2013) 'Meanings are acquired from experiencing differences against a background of sameness, rather than from experiencing sameness against a background of difference: Putting a conjecture to the test by embedding it in a pedagogical tool', *Frontline Learning Research*, 1(1): 24–41. DOI: 10.14786/flr.v1i1.16

Marton, F. and Pong, W.Y. (2005) 'On the unit of description in phenomenography', *Higher Education Research & Development*, 24(4): 335–348. DOI: 10.1080/07294360500284706

Marton, F. and Säljö, R. (1976a) 'On qualitative differences in learning: I – outcome and process', *British Journal of Educational Psychology*, 46(1): 4–11. DOI: 10.1111/j.2044-8279.1976.tb02980.x

Marton, F. and Säljö, R. (1976b) 'On qualitative differences in learning: II – outcome as a function of the learner's conception of the task', *British Journal of Educational Psychology*, 46(2): 115–127. DOI: 10.1111/j.2044-8279.1976.tb02304.x

Marton, F. and Säljö, R. (1997) 'Approaches to learning', in F. Marton, D. Hounsell and N.J. Entwistle (eds) *The Experience of Learning: Implications for and Studying in Higher Education*, second edition, Edinburgh: Scottish Academic Press, pp 39–58.

Marton, F., Carlsson, M. and Halasz, L. (1992) 'Differences in understanding and the use of reflective learning in reading', *British Journal of Educational Psychology*, 62(1): 1–16. DOI: 10.1111/j.2044-8279.1992.tb00995.x

Maybee, C.D. (2006) 'Undergraduate perceptions of information use: The basis for creating user-centred student information literacy instruction', *The Journal of Academic Librarianship*, 32(1): 79–85. DOI: 10.1016/j.acalib.2005.10.010

Maybee, C.D. (2015) *Informed Learning in the Undergraduate Classroom: The Role of Information Shaping Outcomes*, unpublished thesis (PhD), Queensland University of Technology, available at https://eprints.qut.edu.au/89685/4/Clarence_Maybee_Thesis.pdf

McCosker, H., Barnard, A. and Gerber R. (2004) 'Phenomenographic study of women's experiences of domestic violence during the childbearing years', *The Online Journal of Issues in Nursing*, 9(1): 76–88.

McGuigan, N. (2017) *A Phenomenographic Study of Students' Perceptions of Accounting*, unpublished thesis (PhD), University of the West of England, Bristol, available at https://uwe-repository.worktribe.com/output/887380

McKenzie, J.A. (2003) *Variation and Change in University Teachers' Ways of Experiencing Teaching*, unpublished thesis (PhD), University of Technology, Sydney, available at http://hdl.handle.net/10453/20187

McMullin, C. (2023) 'Transcription and qualitative methods: Implications for third sector research', *VOLUNTAS: International Journal of Voluntary and Nonprofit Organizations*, 34(1): 140–153. DOI: 10.1007/s11266-021-00400-3

Miller, J. and Glassner, B. (2011) 'The "inside" and the "outside": Finding realities in interviews', in D. Silverman (ed) *Qualitative Research: Issues of Theory, Method and Practice*, third edition, Los Angeles: SAGE, pp 131–148.

Miller, T. (2017) 'Telling the difficult things: Creating spaces for disclosure, rapport and "collusion" in qualitative interviews', *Women's Studies International Forum*, 61: 81–86. DOI: 10.1016/j.wsif.2016.07.005

Mimirinis, M. and Ahlberg, K. (2021) 'Variation in education doctoral students' conceptions of university teaching', *British Educational Research Journal*, 47(3): 557–578. DOI: 10.1002/berj.3669

Mohd-Ali, S., Puteh-Behak, F., Saat, N.S.M., Darmi, R., Harun, H. and Samah, R. (2016) 'Tackling the issue of credibility in phenomenographic interviewing to capture problem-based learning (PBL) experience', *Mediterranean Journal of Social Sciences*, 7(4): 184–191. DOI: 10.5901/mjss.2016.v7n4p184

Moylan, C.A., Derr, A.S. and Lindhorst, T. (2015) 'Increasingly mobile: How new technologies can enhance qualitative research', *Qualitative Social Work*, 14(1): 36–47. DOI: 10.1177/1473325013516988

Munangatire, T. and McInerney, P. (2022) 'A phenomenographic study exploring the conceptions of stakeholders on their teaching and learning roles in nursing education', *BMC Medical Education*, 22: article number 404. DOI: 10.1186/s12909-022-03392-w

Nelson-Jones, R. (2011) *Six Key Approaches to Counselling and Therapy*, second edition, London: SAGE.

References

Oliver, P. (2003) *The Student's Guide to Research Ethics*, Maidenhead: Open University Press.

Pang, M.F. (2003) 'Two faces of variation: On continuity in the phenomenographic movement', *Scandinavian Journal of Educational Research*, 47(2): 145–156. DOI: 10.1080/00313830308612

Pang, M.F. and Ki, W.W. (2016) 'Revisiting the idea of "critical aspects"', *Scandinavian Journal of Educational Research*, 60(3): 323–336. DOI: 10.1080/00313831.2015.1119724

Patron, E. (2022) *Exploring the Role that Visual Representations Play when Teaching and Learning Chemical Bonding: An Approach Built on Social Semiotics and Phenomenography*, unpublished thesis (PhD), Linnaeus University, available at https://lnu.diva-portal.org/smash/get/diva2:1619343/FULLTEXT01.pdf

Patten, M.L. (2017) *Understanding Research Methods: An Overview of the Essentials*, tenth edition, New York: Routledge.

Patton, M.Q. (2002) *Qualitative Research and Evaluation Methods*, third edition, Thousand Oaks: SAGE.

Perkins, D. (1999) 'The many faces of constructivism', *Educational Leadership*, 57(3): 6–11.

Pickard, A.J. (2007) *Research Methods in Information*, London: Facet Publishing.

Piedra, L.M. (2023) 'Positionality: An analytical building block', *Qualitative Social Work*, 22(4): 611–618. DOI: 10.1177/14733250231183294

Pope, C., Ziebland, S. and Mays, N. (2000) 'Qualitative research in health care: Analysing qualitative data', *British Medical Journal*, 320(7227): 114–116. DOI: https://www.jstor.org/stable/25186804

Rajapakse, G.S. and Kiran, K. (2017) 'The library succession planner's decision-making style', *Library Management*, 38(8/9): 497–510. DOI: 10.1108/LM-02-2017-0017

Reay, T., Zafar, A., Monteiro, P. and Glaser, V. (2019) 'Presenting findings from qualitative research: One size does not fit all!', in T.B. Zilber, J.M. Amis and J. Mair (eds) *The Production of Managerial Knowledge and Organizational Theory: New Approaches to Writing, Producing and Consuming Theory*, Bingley: Emerald Publishing Limited, pp 201–216.

Reed, B. (2006) 'Phenomenography as a way to research the understanding by students of technical concepts', paper presented at *Núcleo de Pesquisa em Tecnologia da Arquitetura e Urbanismo (NUTAU): Technological Innovation and Sustainability*, Sao Paulo, Brazil, pp 1–11.

Richardson, J.T.E. (1999) 'The concepts and methods of phenomenographic research', *Review of Educational Research*, 69(1): 53–82. DOI: 10.3102/00346543069001053

Richardson, J.T.E. (2015) 'Approaches to learning or levels of processing: What did Marton and Säljö (1976a) really say? The legacy of the work of the Göteborg group in the 1970s', *Interchange: A Quarterly Review of Education*, 46(3): 239–269. DOI 10.1007/s10780-015-9251-9

Roberts, K.A. and Wilson, R.W. (2002) 'ICT and the research process: Issues around the compatibility of technology with qualitative data analysis', *Forum Qualitative Sozialforschung/ Forum: Qualitative Social Research*, 3(2): article number 23. DOI: 10.17169/fqs-3.2.862

Robson, C. (1993) *Real World Research*, Oxford and Cambridge, MA: Blackwell.

Rocha-Pinto, S.R.D., Jardim, L.S., Broman, S.L.D.S., Guimaraes, M.I.P. and Trevia, C.F. (2019) 'Phenomenography's contribution to organizational studies based on a practice perspective', *RAUSP Management Journal*, 54(4): 384–398. DOI: 10.1108/ RAUSP-05-2019-0085

Rodríguez Bolívar, M.P. and Alcaide Muñoz, L. (2022) 'Identification of research trends in emerging technologies implementation on public services using text mining analysis', *Information Technology & People*. DOI: 10.1108/ITP-03-2021-0188

Rovio-Johansson, A. and Ingerman, A. (2016) 'Continuity and development in the phenomenography and variation theory tradition', *Scandinavian Journal of Educational Research*, 60(3): 257–271. DOI: 10.1080/00313831.2016.1148074

Salaz, A. (2015) *International Branch Campus Faculty Member Experiences of the Academic Library*, unpublished thesis (Ed.D.), University of Liverpool, available at https://livrepository.liverpool.ac.uk/2010812/3/SalazAli_Apr2015_2010812.pdf

Säljö, R. (1997) 'Talk as data and practice: A critical look at phenomenographic inquiry and the appeal to experience', *Higher Education Research & Development*, 16(2): 173–190. DOI: 10.1080/0729436970160205

Sandberg, J. (1996) 'Are phenomenographic results reliable?', in G. Dall'Alba and B. Hasselgren (eds), *Reflections on Phenomenography: Toward a Methodology?*, Göteborg: Acta Universitatis Gothoburgensis, pp 129–140.

Sandberg, J. (1997) 'Are phenomenographic results reliable?', *Higher Education Research & Development*, 16(2): 203–212. DOI: 10.1080/0729436970160207

Sandberg, J. (2000) 'Understanding human competence at work: An interpretative approach', *The Academy of Management Journal*, 43(1): 9–25. DOI: 10.5465/1556383

Sandelowski, M. and Barroso, J. (2002) 'Finding the findings in qualitative studies', *Journal of Nursing Scholarship*, 34(3): 213–219. DOI: 10.1111/j.1547-5069.2002.00213.x

Seidman, I. (2013) *Interviewing as Qualitative Research: A Guide for Researchers in Education and the Social Sciences*, fourth edition, New York and London: Teachers College, Columbia University.

Shenton, A. and Hayter, S. (2006) 'Terminology deconstructed: Phenomenographic approaches to investigating the term "information"', *Library and Information Science Research*, 28(4): 563–578. DOI: 10.1016/j.lisr.2006.10.003

Sin, S. (2010) 'Considerations of quality in phenomenographic research', *International Journal of Qualitative Methods*, 9(4): 305–319. DOI: 10.1177/160940691000900401

Sjöström, B. and Dahlgren, L.O. (2002) 'Applying phenomenography in nursing research', *Journal of Advanced Nursing*, 40(3): 339–345. DOI: 10.1046/j.1365-2648.2002.02375.x

Smith, J.A. (2008) 'Reflecting on the development of interpretative phenomenological analysis and its contribution to qualitative research in psychology', *Qualitative Research in Psychology*, 1(1): 39–54. DOI: 10.1191/1478088704qp004o

Smith, L. (2015) *Critical Information Literacy and Political Agency: A Critical, Phenomenographic and Personal Construct Study of Young People's Experiences of Political Information*, unpublished thesis (PhD), University of Strathclyde. DOI: 10.48730/r84b-re66

Smith, L. and McMenemy, D. (2016) 'Enhancing agency through information: A phenomenographic exploration of young people's political information experiences', in *Proceedings of the 79th ASIS&T Annual Meeting*, Copenhagen, Denmark, 14–18 October, available at https://pureportal.strath.ac.uk/files/61710 688/Smith_McMenemy_ASIS_T2016_Enhancing_agency_ through_information_a_phenomenographic.pdf

Spencer, L., Ritchie, J., Lewis, J. and Dillon, L. (2003) *Quality in Qualitative Evaluation: A Framework for Assessing Research Evidence*, London: Government Chief Social Researcher's Office, available at https://assets.publishing.service.gov.uk/government/uploads/system/uploads/attachment_data/file/498321/Quality-in-qualitative-evaulation_tcm6-38739.pdf

Stolz, S.A. (2020) 'Phenomenology and phenomenography in educational research: A critique', *Educational Philosophy and Theory*, 52(10): 1077–1096. DOI: 0.1080/00131857.2020.1724088

Stoodley, I., Abdi, E.S., Bruce, C. and Hughes, H. (2018) 'Learning experiences in a giant interactive environment: Insights from The Cube', *Journal of Further and Higher Education*, 42(3): 402–414. DOI: 10.1080/0309877X.2017.1281888

Straub, J.M. (2020) *Pre-Service Teachers' Understanding of Citizenship*, unpublished thesis (PhD), The University of New Brunswick, available at https://unbscholar.dspace.lib.unb.ca/server/api/core/bitstreams/4ad9d0ab-3733-47b0-860d-b26f685d5d98/content

Straub, J.M. and Maynes, N. (2021) 'Rigorous phenomenography: A conceptual model', *Journal of Studies in Education*, 11(2): 71–86. DOI: 10.5296/jse. v11i2.18496

Susskind, R.E. and Susskind, D. (2015) *The Future of the Professions: How Technology will Transform the Work of Human Experts*, Oxford: Open University Press.

Svensson, L. (1977) 'On qualitative differences in learning: III – study skill and learning', *British Journal of Educational Psychology*, 47(3): 233–243. DOI: 10.1111/j.2044-8279.1977.tb02352.x

Svensson, L. (1997) 'Theoretical foundations of phenomenography', *Higher Education Research & Development*, 16(2): 159–171. DOI: 10.1080/0729436970160204

References

Svensson, L. (2016) 'Towards an integration of research on teaching and learning', *Scandinavian Journal of Educational Research*, 60(3): 272–285. DOI: 10.1080/00313831.2015.1120233

Taylor, A. (2017) 'Social work and digitalisation: Bridging the knowledge gaps', *Social Work Education, The International Journal (SWE)*, 36(8): 869–879. DOI: 10.1080/02615479.2017.1361924

Taylor-Beswick, A.M.L. (2019) *Examining the Contribution of Social Work Education to the Digital Professionalism of Students for Practice in the Connected Age*, unpublished thesis (Ed.D.), University of Central Lancashire, available at https://ethos.bl.uk/OrderDetails.do?uin=uk.bl.ethos.784597

Taylor-Beswick, A.M.L. (2023) 'Digitalizing social work education: Preparing students to engage with twenty-first century practice need', *Social Work Education*, 42(1): 44–64. DOI: 10.1080/02615479.2022.2049225

Thomas, G. (2009) *How to Do Research Project*, London: SAGE.

Thunberg, S. and Arnell, L. (2022) 'Pioneering the use of technologies in qualitative research: A research review of the use of digital interviews', *International Journal of Social Research Methodology*, 25(6): 757–768. DOI: 10.1080/13645579.2021.1935565

Tight, M. (nd) *A Phenomenography of Phenomenography*, Lancaster: Lancaster University, available at https://www.lancaster.ac.uk/fass/doc_library/edres/16seminars/tight_01.06.16.pdf

Tight, M. (2016) 'Phenomenography: The development and application of an innovative research design in higher education research', *International Journal of Social Research Methodology*, 19(3): 319–338. DOI: 10.1080/13645579.2015.1010284

Tracy, S.J. (2010) 'Qualitative quality: Eight "big-tent" criteria for excellent qualitative research', *Qualitative Inquiry*, 16(10): 837–851. DOI: 10.1177/1077800410383121

Trem, K. (2017) 'Selecting an appropriate research sample for a phenomenographic study of values', in *UFHRD Conference 2017, 07–09 June 2017, Lisbon, Portugal*, available at https://eprints.leedsbeckett.ac.uk/id/eprint/4096/1/SelectingAnAppropriateResearchSampleAM_TREM.pdf

Trigwell, K. (2000) 'A phenomenographic interview on phenomenography', in J.A. Bowden and E. Walsh (eds) *Phenomenography*, Melbourne: RMIT University Press, pp 62–82.

Trigwell, K. (2006) 'Phenomenography: An approach to research into geography education', *Journal of Geography in Higher Education*, 30(2): 367–372. DOI: 10.1080/03098260600717489

Trigwell, K., Prosser, M. and Ginns, P. (2005) 'Phenomenographic pedagogy and a revised approaches to teaching inventory', *Higher Education Research & Development*, 24(4): 349–360. DOI: 10.1080/07294360500284730

Turner, M. and Noble, K. (2015) 'Phenomenographic elaboration: Arts-based inquiry as a complement to data collection and analysis', in *Proceedings of the Annual International Australian Association for Research in Education Conference (AARE)*, Melbourne: Australian Association for Research in Education, available at https://www.aare.edu.au/data/2015_Conference/Full_papers/285_MichelleTurner.pdf

Uljens, M. (1996) 'On the philosophical foundations of phenomenography', in G. Dall'Alba and B. Hasselgren (eds), *Reflections on Phenomenography: Toward a Methodology?* Göteborg: Acta Universitatis Gothoburgensis, pp 103–128.

Van Rossum, E.J. and Hamer, R. (2010) *The Meaning of Learning and Knowing*, Leiden: Brill.

Venkatasalu, M.R., Kelleher, M. and Shao, C.H. (2015) 'Reported clinical outcomes of high-fidelity simulation versus classroom-based end-of-life care education', *International Journal of Palliative Nursing*, 21(4): 179–186. DOI: 10.12968/ijpn.2015.21.4.179

Visram, S., Goodall, D. and Steven, A. (2014) 'Exploring conceptualizations of knowledge translation, transfer and exchange across public health in one UK region: A qualitative mapping study', *Public Health*, 128(6): 497–503. DOI: 10.1016/j.puhe.2014.02.001

Walsh, E. (2000) 'Phenomenographic analysis of interview transcripts', in J.A. Bowden and E. Walsh (eds) *Phenomenography*, Melbourne: RMIT University Press, pp 19–33.

Wan, S.W.-Y. and Leung, S. (2022) 'Integrating phenomenography with discourse analysis to study Hong Kong prospective teachers' conceptions of curriculum leadership', *Cambridge Journal of Education*, 52(1): 91–116. DOI: 10.1080/0305764X.2021.1946484

Watson, F.A. (2016) 'Lessons learned on approaches to data collection and analysis from a pilot study', *Nurse Researcher*, 24(1): 32–36. DOI: 10.7748/nr.2016.e1444

Watson, F.A. (2019) *Recovery as a Troublesome Concept: A Phenomenographic Study of Mental Health Nursing Students' Learning Experiences*, unpublished thesis (PhD), Durham University, available at http://etheses.dur.ac.uk/13067/1/thesis_final.pdf

Webb, G. (1997) 'Deconstructing deep and surface: Towards a critique of phenomenography', *Higher Education*, 33(2): 95–212. DOI: 10.1023/A:1002905027633

Weber, S. (2008) 'Visual images in research', in J.G. Knowles and A.L. Cole (eds) *Handbook of the Arts in Qualitative Research: Perspectives, Methodologies, Examples and Issues*, London: SAGE, pp 41–53.

Wheeler, E. and McKinney, P. (2015) 'Are librarians' teachers? Investigating academic librarians' perceptions of their own teaching roles', *Journal of Information Literacy*, 9(2): 111–128. DOI: 10.11645/9.2.1985

White, D.S. and Le Cornu, A. (2011) 'Visitors and residents: A new typology for online engagement', *First Monday*, [online] 5 September, available at http://firstmonday.org/ojs/index.php/fm/article/view/3171/3049

Wihlborg, M. (2005) *A Pedagogical Stance on Internationalising Education: An Empirical Study of Swedish Nurse Education from the Perspectives of Students and Teachers*, unpublished thesis (PhD), Lund University, available at https://typeset.io/pdf/a-pedagogical-stance-on-internationalising-education-an-1f8chof01w.pdf

Wiles, R. (2013) *What are Qualitative Research Ethics?* London: Bloomsbury.

Williamson, B. (2021) 'Education technology seizes a pandemic opening', *Current History*, 120(822): 15–20. DOI: 10.1525/curh.2021.120.822.15

Wolcott, H.F. (1994) *Writing Up Qualitative Research*, Newbury Park: SAGE.

Wright, E. and Osman, R. (2018) 'What is critical for transforming higher education? The transformative potential of the pedagogical framework of phenomenography and variation theory of learning for higher education', *Journal of Human Behavior in the Social Environment*, 28(3): 257–270. DOI: 10.1080/10911359.2017.1419898

Yates, C., Partridge, H.L. and Bruce, C.S. (2012) 'Exploring information experiences through phenomenography', *Library and Information Research*, 36(112): 96–119. DOI: 10.29173/lirg496

Yu, S.V. (2019) *From Conceptions to Capacity: Conceptualising the Development of Medical Practitioners' Sense of Being a Doctor and Developing as a Doctor, with Implications for Medical Education*, unpublished thesis (PhD), Australian National University, available at https://openresearch-repository.anu.edu.au/bitstream/1885/185087/6/2019%20Suet%20Voon%20Yu%20Thesis.pdf

Zhao, X. (2015) 'Overseas postgraduates' experience of learning: A phenomenographic study', *Journal of Education and Training*, 2(2): 82–95. DOI: 10.5296/jet.v2i2.7488

Index

A

Åkerlind 4, 5, 9, 13, 20, 21, 22, 23, 24, 25, 29, 31, 32, 43, 47, 49, 57, 61, 63, 75, 76, 77, 78, 84, 85, 86, 87, 92, 93, 94, 95, 96, 97, 107, 110, 111, 117, 118
Ashwin 11, 15, 93, 118
Ashworth 32, 34, 35, 58, 71, 89, 113, 118
awareness 21, 23, 25, 28, 45, 48, 49, 54, 58, 74, 77, 89, 91, 95, 96, 98, 100, 112, 121

B

Booth 4, 18, 21, 22, 24, 25, 26, 27, 28, 48, 54, 57, 67, 92, 94, 98, 103, 105, 110, 112, 119
Bowden 12, 5, 16, 21, 24, 28, 39, 47, 52, 73, 75, 86, 88, 98, 107, 117, 118, 120, 123, 125
Bruce 12, 13, 18, 19, 62, 74, 77, 79, 115, 120, 121

C

categories of description 6, 7, 8, 34, 36, 43, 60, 74, 75, 86, 91, 92, 93, 94, 95, 96, 99, 120
conceptions 6, 12, 15, 16, 18, 19, 24, 25, 26, 28, 34, 37, 48, 49, 52, 54, 56, 57, 60, 63, 65, 73, 74, 76, 88, 101, 103, 105, 106, 107, 112, 119, 122, 123
Cope 3, 116, 121
COVID-19 1, 125

D

data 5, 12, 13, 6, 8, 15, 17, 18, 25, 26, 31, 33, 36, 37, 39, 42, 43, 44, 45, 46, 48, 49, 50, 51, 52, 53, 54, 57, 58, 59, 60, 65, 66, 69, 70, 71, 72, 73, 74, 75, 76, 77, 78, 79, 81, 83, 84, 85, 87, 88, 89, 92, 101, 102, 109, 117, 120
data analysis 5, 25, 37, 42, 60, 69, 71, 72, 73, 74, 75, 77, 79, 81, 83, 85, 87, 89, 109, 117
data generation 5, 8, 31, 44, 51, 52, 53, 59, 65, 66, 74, 109
descriptions of experience 11
dimensions 7, 20, 26, 28, 36, 52, 77, 88, 91, 95, 96, 97, 101, 107, 124
dimensions of variation 7, 20, 26, 28, 77, 95, 96, 97
disciplinary areas 1

E

EAPRIL 9
EARLI 9, 11, 10, 122, 123
early career researchers 2
Entwistle 5, 31, 63, 64, 111, 112, 113, 124
ethics 5, 31, 35, 37, 39, 41, 42, 43, 45, 47, 49, 50, 70, 106, 119, 123, 124

F

findings 5, 13, 8, 17, 20, 23, 34, 45, 48, 49, 50, 60, 63, 87, 88, 89, 91, 92, 93, 95, 97, 101, 102, 103, 105, 107
Focusing activity 6, 55

G

Gerber 19, 118, 125
Green 12, 16, 21, 40, 43, 47, 117, 118, 120, 125

H

hierarchy of categories 6, 100
higher education 1, 2, 5, 9, 17, 110, 113, 117, 119, 122, 124

141

Hornung 3, 4, 8, 10, 21, 35, 36, 41, 43, 48, 58, 61, 62, 64, 79, 80, 81, 82, 83, 84, 85, 86, 87, 88, 95, 96, 97, 98, 99, 100, 102

I

information literacy 18, 19, 20, 102, 103, 118, 119, 120, 124
Ingerman 20, 22, 40, 77, 110, 111, 121, 122
interpretative awareness 8
interview questions 7, 59, 60, 62
Interview schedule 7, 62
interviews 6, 8, 17, 23, 33, 35, 39, 42, 43, 44, 46, 49, 53, 55, 58, 59, 62, 63, 64, 65, 66, 69, 73, 74, 76, 81, 84, 85, 86, 87, 88, 109, 122

J

Jandrić 72

K

Kara 2, 10, 11, 2, 41, 45, 71
Kettunen 28, 50, 112, 122

L

learning 6, 8, 13, 1, 2, 5, 6, 7, 9, 12, 14, 15, 16, 17, 19, 20, 21, 22, 24, 26, 27, 28, 43, 53, 56, 57, 58, 65, 66, 92, 94, 96, 97, 98, 99, 103, 107, 110, 111, 112, 113, 117, 119, 121, 122, 125
Limberg 18, 25, 40
literature 12, 2, 4, 8, 9, 11, 12, 13, 22, 28, 32, 38, 39, 41, 46, 52, 59, 61, 71, 72, 74, 75, 79, 92, 95, 97, 101
Lucas 32, 34, 35, 58, 71, 89, 113, 118
Lupton 81, 102, 103, 104, 116

M

Marton 13, 1, 4, 12, 13, 14, 15, 16, 18, 19, 20, 21, 22, 24, 25, 26, 27, 28, 48, 49, 52, 53, 54, 57, 59, 71, 75, 76, 77, 92, 94, 95, 98, 103, 105, 110, 112, 120, 122, 125

O

origins 1, 5, 11, 12, 13, 55, 109, 110
outcome space 6, 92, 99, 100, 103, 106, 107

P

pedagogy 1, 16, 17, 54
phenomenographer 12, 3, 4, 9, 11, 12, 21, 31, 66, 67, 78, 112, 113
phenomenography 1, 2, 3. 4, 5, 6, 7, 8, 12, 13, 1, 2, 3, 4, 5, 6, 7, 9, 11, 12, 13, 14, 15, 16, 17, 18, 19, 20, 21, 22, 23, 24, 25, 28, 29, 32, 36, 38, 42, 43, 44, 47, 48, 49, 52, 65, 72, 77, 78, 84, 88, 101, 105, 109, 110, 111, 113, 117, 118, 119, 120, 121, 122, 123, 124, 125
Pong 25, 26, 76, 105
professions 2, 19

Q

questioning 3, 60, 62, 63

R

Reed 40, 45, 46, 49, 50, 53, 77, 89, 121
research design 5, 31, 35, 37, 39, 41, 43, 45, 47, 49
research practices 1, 2, 52, 58, 69
research stages 7, 41

S

Säljö 1, 12, 14, 15, 16, 21, 77
Sin 3, 6, 44, 56, 64, 77
social work 8, 5, 7, 19, 21, 36, 55, 57, 93
socio-technical 8, 72
study design 7, 31, 32, 35, 36, 38, 39
Svensson 12, 14, 15, 21, 110

T

Taylor-Beswick 3, 4, 8, 10, 2, 35, 37, 39, 55, 56, 57, 70, 71, 72, 73, 79, 89, 92, 93, 94, 95, 119, 125
technology 2, 69, 70, 86, 118, 122
Tight 3, 5, 6, 53, 91, 95, 97, 121
transcription 5, 31, 34, 58, 69, 70, 71, 72, 73, 74, 75, 77, 79, 81, 83, 85, 87, 89, 120
Trigwell 17, 25, 39

V

vignettes 7, 101, 102

W

Webber 3, 5, 11, 12

www.ingramcontent.com/pod-product-compliance
Lightning Source LLC
Chambersburg PA
CBHW071713020426
42333CB00017B/2252